Martin Dunford

T0270455

111 Places
in Norwich
That You
Shouldn't Miss

Photographs by Karin Tearle

emons:

This book is dedicated to Sonny,
with whom I walked many miles.

© Emons Verlag GmbH
All rights reserved
© Photographs by Karin Tearle
Norwich Puppet Theatre (ch. 64): Puppets from Norwich Puppet Theatre's
2022 production of *Cinderella* created by Mark Mander. Puppets and costumes
designed by Mark Mander and made by Keith Frederick.
© Cover icon: shutterstock.com/Helen Hotson
Layout: Editorial Design & Art Direction, Conny Laue,
based on a design by Lübbeke | Naumann | Thoben
Maps: altancicek.design, www.altancicek.de
Basic cartographical information from Openstreetmap,
© OpenStreetMap-Mitwirkende, OdbL
Editing: Martin Sketchley
Printing and binding: Grafisches Centrum Cuno, Calbe
Printed in Germany 2023
ISBN 978-3-7408-1733-6
First edition

Guidebooks for Locals & Experienced Travellers
Join us in uncovering new places around the world at
www.111places.com

Foreword

'What a grand, higgledy-piggledy, sensible old place Norwich is!'
J. B. Priestley

Tucked away in its own corner of eastern England, Norwich has a thoroughly undeserved reputation for provincialism. It's supposedly a quiet, forgotten sort of place, but in fact the reverse is true. Like the surrounding county of Norfolk, Norwich is not on the way to anywhere and is not close to any other major urban centres. But that doesn't make Norwich a backwater; rather it's a self-sufficient city, firmly rooted in its region, with an almost belligerent sense of pride. Scratch the surface and you will find a city full of creative, forward-looking people who would rather be in Norwich than anywhere else – something reflected in an unusually high quota of thriving independent shops, pubs and restaurants.

Once England's second city, Norwich is also a city of historical layers, just waiting to be unwrapped, a curious mixture of medieval streets and houses, 1960s mistakes and Victorian grandeur, all cleverly re-purposed for the modern age. It may seem like an odd comparison, but Norwich is like Rome, with something of historical significance in every building, brick and pavement crack, and usually a story to tell, too. Significantly, the city once had a church for every week of the year and a pub for every day. It doesn't have those numbers now but it's still a city of churches, home not only to one of England's greatest Norman cathedrals but also the densest concentration of medieval churches in the world, and its pubs remain one of its greatest pleasures. But there is so much else besides. Uncovering the secrets of Norwich's ancient centre while enjoying its considerable modern-day pleasures has been both a revelation and a pleasure. I hope that in this book I've uncovered a few places and stories of which both residents and regular visitors are unaware. For everyone else, Norwich – 'City of Stories' – is waiting.

111 Places

1 The Adam & Eve

The oldest pub in a city of ancient pubs

Tucked away in the ancient streets to the east of the cathedral, the Adam & Eve is the oldest pub in a city of ancient pubs – indeed, Norwich used to claim to have a pub for every day of the year, although it now has around half that. The Adam & Eve has been here for around 750 years, believed to have been founded in 1249 on the site of an old Saxon well, which still exists under the main floor of the pub.

The flint and brick building, adorned at each end by Dutch-style gables, one stepped, the other curved, was originally a small brewery tap managed by monks, and was used as a watering hole by labourers working on the city's cathedral. It also supplied ale to the patients of the Great Hospital next door. Later, it was the scene of violent skirmishes during the infamous Kett Rebellion of 1549, and is said to harbour the ghost of a local landowner murdered by rebels on the premises. Various monks are also said to haunt the place, including one whose remains were discovered under the floorboards in the 1970s. Later, local 19th-century serial killer James Rush is said to have been a regular here, plotting his dire deeds at one of its tables. This was presumably across the bar from another famous regular, the author George Borrow, who attended nearby Norwich School and wrote lovingly of Norwich between penning his tales of travel throughout Europe.

So much for the history – but what sort of place is the Adam & Eve now? Well, it's a good place to sit outside and enjoy a pint on a summer evening, that's for sure; and also the ideal place to arrange a meeting, because everyone in Norwich knows where it is. Inside there are two low-ceilinged bars, both very cosy, and the pub serves good local ales and decent food. Overall, it remains a refreshingly unpretentious place for a drink, and relatively tourist-free, despite its eminent history.

Address 17 Bishopgate, Norwich NR3 1RZ, +44 (0)1603 667423 | **Getting there** Bus to Tombland; 10-minute walk from the railway station following Riverside Road, crossing the Bishop Bridge and following Bishopgate | **Hours** Mon–Sat 11am–11pm, Sun noon–10.30pm | **Tip** The Adam & Eve is not a bad place to start a cycle tour following the route of the brand-new 'Rebellion Way', a 200-mile route around Norfolk that heads from the pub across the river and up to Mousehold Heath before heading out of the city.

2 Alan Partridge Mural
Norwich's best-known fictional creation

Perhaps the most famous denizen of Norwich is a fictional one: Alan Partridge, the extraordinary, self-obsessed, fatuous and almost always hilarious comic creation of comedian Steve Coogan. Partridge's image appears on an outside wall of the Anglia Square car park, just off Magdalen Street. He's seen in full OTT presenter mode, with his signature beneath. Created by one David 'Gnasher' Nash, the mural is essential viewing for any Partridge fan.

Partridge was 'born' in the early 1990s, having featured as a sports reporter in the satirical radio show *On the Hour* and then in his own spoof chat show, *Knowing Me, Knowing You*. Both shows transferred to TV in 1994, and Partridge found a much wider audience, later spawning the comedy *I'm Alan Partridge*, which ran for five years and won two BAFTA awards, and another show – *Mid-Morning Matters* – which was similarly successful. However, the pinnacle of Partridge's success was perhaps the 2013 feature film *Alpha Papa*. This was partly filmed in Norwich and Norfolk, and famously premiered at Anglia Square's Hollywood cinema – now closed.

Alan is inextricably bound up with Norwich and Norfolk: in the film he works for North Norfolk Digital Radio, while at one point he also presents a show for Radio Norwich, and was so synonymous with the city that a statue of him was briefly erected outside The Forum a couple of years ago. Opinions are divided as to whether Partridge has been good for Norwich or not, but it doesn't seem to have done the city much harm, even when he took a tour of the county in a one-off TV mockumentary, *Welcome to the Places of My Life*. In this programme he introduces viewers to 'East Anglia, the Plump Peninsula, Home of the Broads… the Wales of the East… Norfolk', channels Hitler on a visit to City Hall, and takes a tour of Norwich Market, snaffling as much free food as he can.

Address Anglia Square, Magdalen Street, Norwich NR3 1DZ | Getting there Multiple buses go past Anglia Square and up and down Magdalen Street; 15–20-minute walk from the railway station | Hours Visible 24 hours | Tip In a 'Knowing Me, Knowing You' Christmas episode, Alan tours Norwich, jogging through the cathedral cloisters and visiting the old Norwich & Norfolk Hospital before it moved out of town.

3 Amelia Opie

'Mrs Opie, Norwich is my lawful and proper designation'

Was there ever as shocking a woman in the early 19th century as Amelia Opie? A poet, novelist and fiery abolitionist, her racy novels dealt with issues of female sexuality before such a thing was acknowledged to exist. Born in Norwich in 1769, Amelia Opie died there 84 years later, having written over a dozen works of fiction and poetry. She was a prominent Quaker and a member of the anti-slavery movement, but most of all she was a well-connected intellectual, a friend of fellow Norwich native Elizabeth Fry, as well as influential thinkers and dissenters such as Mary Wollstonecraft and her second husband, the philosopher William Godwin.

Married to the accomplished and successful Norwich portrait painter, John Opie, Amelia's first novel, *The Dangers of Coquetry*, was published anonymously in 1791. She went on to publish many novels under her married name, however, which were mostly very well received. Her 1801 novel *Father and Daughter* was much admired by Sir Walter Scott, among other luminaries. She also published several volumes of poetry and a biography of her husband. A lovely portrait of Amelia painted by John hangs in the National Portrait Gallery.

Amelia Opie is now remembered in the name of the diminutive street that connects Castle Meadow with London Street in the city centre – a street that was once the centre of Norwich's red light district, and went by the somewhat unfortunate name of 'Gropecunt Lane'. We have to assume the area had become considerably more respectable by the mid-19th century, as Amelia was resident in the house on the corner of Castle Meadow at the time of her death in 1853. A plaque on the side of the house remembers her as 'Authoress, Dramatist, Poetess and brilliant Conversationalist' – which would seem to be the sort of elegy this prominent and distinguished author would have been very happy with.

Address Opie Street, Norwich NR1 3DP | Getting there Bus to Castle Meadow; 10-minute walk from the railway station | Hours Always accessible | Tip After viewing the plaque, stop off for an ice cream at Opie Street's excellent and authentic Café Gelato, which has a statue of Opie on its roof! Amelia is also remembered by her simple grave in the Gildencroft Quaker Burial Ground off Chatham Street in NR3.

4 Anna Sewell Memorial

Black Beauty author commemorated

A native of Great Yarmouth, the author of Black Beauty in fact lived much of her life in London, but it's in Norwich that Anna Sewell spent the last years of her life and here she is best remembered. As a child, she came to the city and to Norfolk often, visiting her grandparents in Buxton, where she learned to ride, and it was here that she wrote her famous book, shortly before her death in 1878 at the age of 58.

Anna Sewell's mother Mary was a children's author, but unfortunately her daughter was often ill, and crippled for much of her life after an accident as a teenager. The Sewells moved to Old Catton, on the fringes of the city, in 1871, partly because of Anna's failing health but also to be near her brother Philip, who was recently widowed. It was here that she began work on *Black Beauty*, or 'The Autobiography of a Horse' as it was sub-titled. The book drew on her love of her horses and her wish to expose the various cruelties to which they were often exposed. Mostly bed-ridden during these years, she spent around five years working on the book, which was eventually published by Jarrolds in 1877 (see ch. 46), just five months before she died. It quickly became a classic, read by both adults and children, and is still in print today, having sold around 50 million copies and inspired around a dozen film and TV adaptations.

It's a rather sad story, and partly because of that and the enduring popularity of her one and only book, Sewell is remembered in a number of ways in Norwich, in particular on the land once owned by Anna's brother Philip, just north of the city centre. Here, the entrance to the triangular Sewell Park is marked by a memorial water trough, now filled with flowers, which was placed here in 1917 by Anna's cousin Ada Sewell. A short walk north from here, the Sewell Barn Theatre is said to have once housed the horse that inspired Black Beauty.

Address Junction of Constitution Hill and St Clement's Hill, Norwich NR3 4BA | Getting there Turquoise Bus 13 towards Old Catton and Spixworth goes right by. | Hours 24 hours | Tip Anna is buried in the Quaker Cemetery in Lamas, next door to Buxton, around nine miles north, where a memorial is set into the wall of what is now a private home.

5 Arminghall Arch

Hidden secrets of Norwich Magistrates Court

Norwich is a city of layers. Its buildings have been built on top of each other over the years, and many display relics from multiple eras within their walls. Norwich Magistrates Court is a great example: situated in one of the most historic parts of the city, right next door to the cathedral, it's a bland modern building on the outside, and gives no hint of the treasures that lie within.

One of these is The Arminghall Arch, and fortunately it's very easy to see: just show up at the main entrance and ask to see the arch, which is located on the first floor. A beautifully carved archway dating from the 14th century, it's rather unsympathetically displayed amid the brightly lit corridors of the offices. It's a well-travelled piece of stone – made in 1320 for the Carmelite Friary across the river, and a couple of hundred years later finding its way to Arminghall Hall to the south of Norwich, where it was incorporated into the façade of what was then a brand-new country house. When the hall was demolished, the arch returned to Norwich and the Crown Point seat of the Colman family, later being acquired by the city and ending up here – overall, a rather unspectacular end to what was by any standards an epic journey.

Perhaps more impressive are the flint remains of the undercroft of an 11th-century house, discovered during an archaeological dig before construction of the current building in the 1980s. The house – which would have faced the river behind and been an impressive family residence – was perhaps home to an official from the neighbouring cathedral, which was being built at the same time. Beneath a trapdoor, a spiral staircase leads down to the ruins, which include two-metre-high walls, a couple of doorways and – perhaps most interesting of all – the remains of a Norman toilet that would have discharged into the river beyond!

Address Bishopgate, Norwich NR3 1UP | **Getting there** Bus to Tombland; 10-minute walk from the railway station | **Hours** Arminghall Arch Mon–Fri 9am–5pm. The Norman house is usually open on Heritage Open Days in September. | **Tip** The village of Arminghall lies a few miles south of Norwich close to the Roman site of Caistor St Edmund (see ch. 18), and is best known for the so-called 'Arminghall Henge', a prehistoric timber circle that was discovered in the 1920s and recently excavated.

6 __ The Assembly House

Elegant building revitalised by celebrity chef

One of Norwich's most elegant buildings, and bang in the city cen-tre, The Assembly House was originally the site of a medieval church and seminary, St Mary in the Fields (which gave its name to the nearby Chapelfield development) – a plaque found in excavations dates back to 1454 and is mounted on the wall. A series of houses were built on the site over subsequent centuries, and the current building was constructed in the mid-18th century by Thomas Ivory (architect of the Octagon Chapel) as a place to stage events – balls, public meetings, concerts and musical evenings – hosting Paganini and Franz Liszt among many others. Later the building was bought by the Girls' Day School Trust, and was the home of Norwich High School until the 1930s. It then fell into disrepair, and suffered a dev-astating fire in the mid-1990s.

Thankfully, The Assembly House was raised from the dead in the late 1990s, and now prospers under the assured guidance of local celebrity chef Richard Hughes and his wife Stacia. It's now a res-taurant, cookery school, wedding venue and boutique hotel – with a bit of exhibition space and the odd business meeting thrown in for good measure – and is remarkably well suited to all these things. The stuccoed central hall is one of Norwich's grandest spaces, and it's a pleasure just to pass the time here sipping a coffee and watching the world go by. There's a lovely space for a wedding just off here, and plenty of room outside the front of the building for summer over-flows and mingling, while on the other side of the main hall, the rather grand restaurant offers an excellent lunch menu in a spectac-ular setting. A delicious afternoon tea really does the room justice, with a multi-tiered selection of beautifully presented savouries, sand-wiches and pastries. For those with a less sweet tooth, there's also the option of 'afternoon cheese' instead!

Address Theatre Street, Norwich NR2 1RQ, +44 (0)1603 626402, www.assemblyhousenorwich.co.uk | Getting there Buses 21 and 22 stop right outside; 15-minute walk from the railway station | Hours Open for breakfast daily 9–11.30am, lunch & afternoon tea noon–3.30pm | Tip The rest of the building is given over to 15 beautiful boutique guest bedrooms on either side of the central garden, making this one of the best and most convenient places to stay in Norwich.

7 — Augustine Steward's House

Norwich's wonkiest, most historic house

Norwich is a city stacked full of ancient crooked houses, but a good contender for the wonkiest of them all is a three-storey house on Tombland: located directly opposite the cathedral's Erpingham Gate, the so-called Augustine Steward House is a half-timbered property built in the 1530s – though some records say it was built in 1504. Whenever it was built, the house is a fairly typical medieval merchant's residence, built for both commerce, with an undercroft in the basement, and with mullioned windows projecting from its residential upper floors.

Steward was a very well-to-do local merchant who served as sheriff and later mayor, and who funded many of the city's buildings during the 16th century. He died in 1571, and is buried in the nearby church of St Peter Hungate, but his merchant's mark remains visible on the corner of the building. Take a walk through Tombland Alley to admire the building from outside, and follow the path up past the church of St George (see ch. 88).

The house is perhaps best known as a venue for negotiations between government troops and the rebels during the Kett's Rebellion in the summer of 1549 (see ch. 49), when Steward hosted talks between the Marquis of Northampton and Robert Kett – as a result of which, the house was later attacked by some of Kett's followers. Later, the Earl of Warwick, who eventually defeated the rebels on 27 August 1549, had his headquarters here. It's no surprise that the building is allegedly haunted – in this case by a young girl in grey, who was locked up in the house in the 1570s after it was sealed off because its inhabitants had all died of the plague. The story goes that the girl in question had herself survived the Black Death – but was forced to eat her family in an effort to stay alive! Whether this gruesome tale is true or not, 14 Tombland is just the sort of house to encourage such stories!

Address 14 Tombland, Norwich NR3 1HF | Getting there Purple Line buses to Tombland; 10–15-minute walk from the railway station | Hours Not open to the public | Tip The only way to gain access to the Augustine Steward House is by visiting 'Cryptic Escape' – an escape room that occupies its lower floors; the entrance is around the corner on Tombland Alley.

8 Bawburgh Village

Pretty riverside village and shrine to a saint

Around five miles to the west of Norwich, Bawburgh is one of the most picturesque villages situated within the sway of the city – just across the A47, right on the river Yare, which meanders west towards its source near Mattishall. Bawburgh has an idyllic riverside location, and would be worth visiting to enjoy that alone. But it also has an excellent pub in the King's Head, which occupies one of its most historic buildings in the centre of the village, so you can rest up here for a while too – either enjoying a meal or an overnight stay.

In truth, there's not much to do in Bawburgh, but the river is lovely and abuts the village green, and there are a number of ancient buildings dotted along the main street, including the late 16th-century Blacksmiths Cottage and Old Post Office at the far end. The mill straddling the river has been here since the days of the Domesday Book, but the current structure dates from the 19th century and – like most other properties here – is now a private residence.

The village is a good springboard for country walks, and you should at least try a stroll up to the church of St Mary and St Walstan, which looks down on Bawburgh from a ridge above. It's one of Norfolk's 124 round-towered churches, dating from the early 14th century. Said to have been born in Bawburgh, St Walstan is a little-known saint outside Norfolk but a useful one locally, in that he is the patron saint of farming and farmworkers. Although said to have been of noble birth, he preferred to work as a farm labourer, and this church is essentially his shrine. Walstan was the centre of a humble but important cult during the Middle Ages, when Bawburgh was a place of regular pilgrimage: he is said to have died mid-prayer in 1016 and was buried on this site, having been carried here by two mystical calves. A well sprung up where he was laid, and the church was subsequently built to mark the spot.

Address Bawburgh, Norwich NR9 | **Getting there** By car, a 20-minute drive from central Norwich following Dereham Road out of town – no buses stop there. | **Hours** Always accessible | **Tip** The King's Head is a cosy foodie pub with two AA rosettes, and was shortlisted as East of England 'Pub of the Year' in 2022. It's well worth venturing to for both drinks – real ales from the Fakenham Barsham Brewery and Norwich's Mr Winters – and good gastropub food; rooms are also available for those who want to stay longer.

9 — Benedicts

Shut your eyes, taste the food…you're in Norwich

It's not just the Delia effect: Norwich has become a city of foodies in the past decade or so, nowhere more so than in The Lanes, which harbours several excellent eateries within its peaceful precincts. One of the best of these – Benedicts – has been based in a former tailors on Benedict Street since 2015, offering beautifully presented Modern British food cooked by Norwich native Richard Bainbridge.

Before this, Bainbridge worked for four years with Michel Roux Snr at the Waterside Inn in Bray, then under Galton Blackiston at Morston Hall in North Norfolk – both Michelin-starred establishments that have clearly left their mark at Benedicts, and not just with regard to the food: the service too is top-notch, delivered by a small committed staff that clearly identifies with the mission of Richard and his Katja to open their ideal restaurant. In a nutshell, this is a friendly place serving delicious food made using accessible local ingredients, in the belief that restaurants should be places to forget the world for a couple of hours, eating food that is special but at the same time without frills. There's also a touch of nostalgia to the dishes, with throwbacks such as prawn cocktail evoking taste sensations and family food experiences from Bainbridge's childhood that may strike a chord in you too.

So while Benedicts may sound like a regular neighbourhood restaurant, it most definitely isn't. However, although the restaurant itself is stylishly low-key, it's far from being a shrine to fine dining. It serves a good-value set lunch menu twice a week, and a choice of reasonably priced tasting menus in the evening. Dishes change every four to five weeks, and are entirely guided by what's seasonal and available locally. The point is, Bainbridge insists, that you should be able to shut your eyes and tell not only that you are in Norfolk, but what season it is too.

Address 9 St Benedict Street, Norwich NR2 4PE, +44 (0)1603 926080, www.restaurantbenedicts.com | Getting there Five-minute walk from Market Place; 15–20-minute walk from the railway station | Hours Lunch Fri & Sat noon–2pm; Dinner Tue–Sat 5–10pm | Tip Footsteps away on St Benedict Street, The Plough is a good complement to Benedicts' 'all things Norfolk' philosophy – it's the Norwich brewpub of south Norfolk's Grain Brewery, and a good place for a drink before or after your meal.

10 BeWILDerwood

Sustainable adventure park for kids of all ages

Just outside the Broadland village of Horning, around 10 miles from Norwich, BeWILDerwood is one of the largest attractions close to the city, a deliberately sustainable theme park based on a series of books for children by local author and landowner Tom Blofeld that were inspired by the watery world of the Broads. With a fun, nostalgic freshness to the place, it's extremely popular during school holidays and throughout the summer, but its mixture of fantasy and adventure has something for kids of all ages.

The park was set up by Tom and a couple of his mates around 15 years ago, in an area of marshy woodland owned by his family – the Blofelds are one of the oldest families hereabouts, and own much of the land between Horning and Wroxham. You'll find plenty of memorials to them in the local church. If the name seems familiar, it's because Ian Fleming went to school with Tom Blofeld's uncle, immortalising the surname as that of the villain in his James Bond stories. BeWILDerwood is a theme park, but one that's deliberately different to any other, aiming above all to bring the waterscape of the Broads to life for kids. It's both a land of make-believe based on characters in Blofeld's books, and an oversized adventure playground, with rope bridges and ladders, treehouses, slides and zip-wires, all connected by boardwalks and accessible, mostly wheelchair-friendly forest paths. There are boat rides, a 'sky maze', face-painting and story-telling, and plenty to keep kids from toddlers to teens occupied for hours. It has a policy of sustainability too, with everything made of wood, rope and other ecologically sound resources – although the undeniable wholesomeness of it all harks back to an age before such things seemed important. The park has proven so successful that in recent years a second BeWILDerwood has opened at Bickley Moss in Cheshire.

Address Horning Road, Hoveton St John, Norfolk NR12 8JW, www.norfolk.bewilderwood.co.uk | **Getting there** Regular buses to Horning that run right by BeWILDerwood; train to Wroxham & Hoveton, then a five-minute taxi ride; by car, a 25-minute drive from central Norwich | **Hours** See the website for current information on visiting | **Tip** After visiting BeWILDerwood why not visit nearby Burnt Fen Alpacas, where you can stroll around a private broad with a herd of alpacas, enjoy a cream tea and even join a weaving and spinning class using the alpacas' wool.

11 Bishop's Garden

Bucolic secret in the heart of the city

Norwich is full of secret gardens and hidden open spaces, but probably the most spectacular of all are the four acres of the Bishop's Garden. This magnificent display of flora lies immediately north of the Bishop's Palace, and is open to visitors on selected Sundays during the summer months.

Parts of the garden date back to the 1100s, when Bishop Herbert de Losinga built the first palace here, making the gardens as historic as just about anywhere Norwich has to offer – not to mention a thoroughly peaceful haven, located right in the centre of the city. Extended during the 14th century by Bishop John Salmon, and still bordered by the high flint walls that were added then, the gardens incorporate the ruins of a medieval hall built by Bishop Salmon – what's left is known as Bishop Salmon's Porch. They also offer good views not only of the Norman north transept of the cathedral, but also of Norwich School, which occupies the original Bishop's Palace, and the 17th-century chapel that now serves as the school's library. These days the bishop occupies a more modern 1950s building located near the garden's entrance.

Meticulously kept by two full-time gardeners, the garden still conforms to a plan laid out around three centuries ago. There are beautiful long herbaceous borders, a mini woodland walk, a herb garden and a wildflower meadow, as well as a fertile kitchen garden planted with an abundance of organic produce. There's also a formal rose garden bordered by box hedges and various other beds with sub-tropical and other abundant shrubs. There are even a few bee hives, and a spreading hebe grown from a cutting taken from Queen Victoria's wedding bouquet. Afterwards, you can take the weight off your feet, relax and treat yourself to tea and homemade cakes at the garden's own café, and maybe also buy a plant or two.

Address Palace Plain, Norwich NR3 1SB | Getting there Purple Line buses to Tombland; 15-minute walk from the railway station | Hours Open two Sundays each month May–Aug 1–4.30pm | Tip Keen gardeners can buy shrubs at the small plant nursery, with all proceeds going to a variety of charities chosen by the bishop each summer.

12 Book Hive

Beautiful and inspirational literary shop

Norwich's favourite bookshop has been in existence since 2009, when Henry Layte – a jobbing actor and writer living in London – returned to his home county of Norfolk, looking for something to support what he thought might be a burgeoning writing career. Between jobs and enjoying his lunch on a London Street bench one day, he noticed the former florist on the corner of St Andrew's Hill was empty, and thought it the perfect place for a bookshop – an idea that changed his life forever.

Henry's venture has gone from strength to strength, not only forging a reputation as a brilliantly curated independent bookstore, but as a publisher and literary impresario, too. His publishing company, Galley Beggar, discovered and published the experimental novel *A Girl is a Half-Formed Thing* by Eimar McBride, which won the Women's Prize for Fiction in 2014, and he continues to publish new and undiscovered fiction and non-fiction, much of it from Norwich and Norfolk, under his Propolis imprint, which includes Poet Laureate Simon Armitage among its writers. Norfolk-loving Canadian veteran Margaret Atwood finished her *Heart Goes Last* novel in the writers' booths Henry rents out upstairs, and the shop basically acts as the hub of Norwich's literary scene.

Book Hive is the bookshop Henry wanted to create rather than one he thought would be a financial success. Happily, it is both – a small bookshop appealing to book lovers and literary adventurers looking for something to read, but not necessarily sure what they want, with a carefully chosen selection of books of all genres across two floors. Curation is inevitable in such a tight space, but it's done beautifully. It's difficult to visit without buying something from this inspirational store, which is expertly run by Henry and his team. It's the exact opposite of the large chains and online stores, and much the better for it.

Address 53 London Street, Norwich NR2 1HL, +44 (0)1603 219268, www.thebookhive.co.uk |
Getting there Bus to Castle Meadow; 10–15-minute walk from the railway station | Hours
Mon 10am–5.30pm, Tue–Sat 9.30am–5.30pm, Sun 11am–4pm | Tip As well as a book, why
not pick up if you can a bit of Book Hive 'merch'? Their mugs are proudly inscribed with quotes
about the shop, ranging from Margaret Atwood's 'Eclectic, thoughtful, tempting, a must
for book lovers visiting Norwich' to – Henry's favourite – Michael Gove's 'Illiberal Bigots'.

13 Bread Source

Artisanal bakery locals wouldn't be without

Although barely a decade old, Bread Source has already become one of Norwich's most essential businesses, the one place that the city's denizens really couldn't do without. Luckily, the city has several branches of this artisanal bakery, which offers its own selection of scrumptious wares. Founded in 2012 by local baker Steven Winter and his wife Hannah, the first Bread Source bakery was located in Norfolk's official 'Slow Food' town, Aylsham. Success has been such that they have since moved the establishment to larger premises, and there are now no fewer than five branches in Norwich – the largest of which is on Upper St Giles Street.

Naturally, the jewel in Bread Source's crown is indeed bread. This is produced in the traditional way, using high quality flour and natural yeast, with salt and water the only other additional ingredients. Although artisan bread is available pretty much everywhere these days, there is undeniably something rather special about the stuff produced at Bread Source – crusty white tin loafs, superb sourdough bloomers, fruit bread and rye loaves, ciabattas and baguettes – all of which are quite simply delicious. In collaboration with local craft brewer Ampersand, they even sell a beer made with their leftover bread – the delightfully named 'Brew Loaf Story'.

In addition, the Bread Source shops offer a variety of both sweet and savoury items in their windows that are guaranteed to tempt even the most waistline-wary passers-by – featuring products such as herby sausage rolls, unctuous treacle tarts, sticky and soft cinnamon buns, and the lightest and flakiest of croissants. Grab something to go or perch on a stool inside and enjoy whatever takes your fancy, while sipping a cup of their equally excellent coffee. Whichever way you look at it, Bread Source is one of Norwich's most important foodie pleasures.

Address 93 Upper St Giles Street, Norwich NR2 1AB, plus branches on Bridewell Alley, Magdalen Street, Norwich Market, the Cathedral Refectory, and at the bakery itself on Marriott Close | Getting there Five-minute walk from Market Place; 15-minute walk from the railway station | Hours Mon–Sat 7.30am–6pm, Sun 8am–4pm; other branch hours vary | Tip There's another Norwich bakery and café that's worthy of mention – Two Magpies – but this one originated in Suffolk, and has since spread across East Anglia, with branches in Woodbridge, Aldeburgh and Southwold, right up to Holt in North Norfolk. The Norwich branch, on Timber Hill, is open every day, and serves a superb array of fresh bread, sweet and savoury pastries, cakes and coffee.

14 __ Brick Pizza

On a sunny day you could be in Naples

You're spoilt for choice for food around Norwich's Market Place, but there's one place in particular that you'll always go back to: Brick Pizza. Tucked away in a corner in the shadow of the church of St Peter Mancroft (see ch. 94), this establishment serves what is arguably the city's best pizza, in an environment that feels like the ultimate Italian street pizzeria: tiny, friendly and a without-ceremony vibe where the focus is on the pizza.

The pizza here is Neapolitan style, which means the dough is made with extremely finely milled flour and kneaded by hand, and the pizzas are thin and crispy but have a thickish, often slightly charred crust. It's pretty special – the dough is given ample time to rise after being rolled out and is then baked very quickly – for perhaps just for a minute or two – at a high temperature in a wood-burning oven, just as pizza should be! Neapolitan aficionados – and the guys at Brick Pizza! – claim that the slow rising of the dough and the speed of cooking make for a better flavour.

The oven here operates at 500 degrees, which explains why it's impossible to cook authentic pizza at home. Instead, make the most of the pizza they serve here and be sure to eat the crusts. It's all cooked in front of you, and toppings include the Neapolitan classic Margherita, Napoli (with anchovies) and the most authentic of them all, the Marinara – just tomatoes and garlic. They also offer lots of toppings you would never see in Naples, for example the Hawaiinot (with, yes, pineapple and ham) as well as numerous fried snacks and other goodies.

Be prepared to wait for a table – this really is a small establishment! – or just get a takeaway and eat it at one of the benches in the churchyard or on the market. Alternatively, grab a drink at The Garnet and enjoy your pizza at one of their outdoor tables. On a sunny day you could almost be in Naples!

Address 39 Market Place, Norwich NR2 1ND, +44 (0)1603 620661, www.brickpizza-norwich.co.uk | **Getting there** 10-minute walk from the railway station, and plenty of buses stop nearby | **Hours** Daily noon–10pm | **Tip** Brick Pizza also does pasta, at the rather wonderful, equally small restaurant, Yard, across the market square on Pottergate. Go there for an authentic bucatini cacio e pepe or pappardelle with ragu washed down with a cheeky cocktail.

15 __ The Bridewell Museum

Treasure-trove of artefacts tell tale of Norwich

Housed in a building that served as the city's prison from 1585, the Museum of Norwich at The Bridewell is one of a handful of museums worth visiting. It offers a well-presented and fascinating treasure-trove of artefacts that tell Norwich's story.

The Bridewell was replaced as Norwich's gaol in 1828, when a new, larger complex was built on the outskirts of the city, on the site of the current Roman Catholic cathedral. It's not given to spacious and lavish displays, but is brilliantly done, with a fascinating cascade of often workaday artefacts right up to the 20th century. These convey a massive sense of time passing, and how ordinary people's lives were affected by change.

The ground floor focuses on a time when Norwich was England's second city, and the textile industry and other trades were making many people very rich. There's lots of fascinating detail on the retail trades, the cloth industry, as well as its time as a prison. Look out for the weird Norwich fable of 'Peter the Wild Boy' – a mysterious, feral child from Germany who turned up in Norwich one day and was imprisoned here – then visit the nearby Wild Man pub, which remembers him.

The first floor has more on the city's industrial past. For all the city's quaintness, for centuries before the Industrial Revolution, Norwich was an economic powerhouse, with a busy port and factories devoted to textiles, engineering and footwear, which took hold as weaving declined and made Norwich the country's foremost shoemaking centre. Displays include a loom from the days of the textile industry, items relating to the Colman family and their mustard business, and the Start-Rite kids' shoe brand, making footwear in the city since 1792. The brewing business gets a mention too, quite rightly in a city that once had more than 500 pubs. Sections on Norwich City and the post-war years conclude the collection.

Address Bridewell Alley, Norwich NR2 1AQ, www.museums.norfolk.gov.uk | Getting there Purple Line buses stop near the Bridewell; 15-minute walk from the railway station | Hours Tue – Sat 10am – 4.30pm | Tip Join one of the monthly tours of the Bridewell's Undercroft, an atmospheric vaulted space that once formed the ground floor of the original merchant's – later the mayor's – house that stood on this site and pre-dates even the prison.

16 Britons Arms

One of the oldest buildings in Norwich

Elm Hill is a picturesque street, but its oldest building steals most of its thunder. A thatched and whitewashed structure from the early 1400s, the Britons Arms is a Norwich landmark, not only because it's one of the oldest buildings in a city of very old buildings, but because for years it was the city's most famous tearoom, run for almost half a century by sisters Gilly Mixer and Sue Skipper. It remains basically a café and tea room, but the sisters retired a couple of years ago, with local chef Richard Ellis taking over in 2021. He has added more of a dining flavour, serving a varied and imaginative lunch menu every day, and dinner three evenings a week.

A nice place for both a cuppa and a piece of cake, and an excellent dinner, it's also a truly fascinating building, the only one on Elm Hill to have survived a devastating fire in 1507. It's thought to have been built as a 'beguinage' – a phenomenon more common in the Low Countries in the Middle Ages, where lay women lived together in a Christian community, but not as full-blown nuns. At some point it's also believed to have housed visiting students from the seminary on the site of what is now the Assembly House.

Richard is happy to conduct quick tours of the building, time permitting, and to show you around what would have been quite an advanced building for its time, with three storeys of two rooms each, heated by their own fireplaces and connected by a staircase to the side. Some parts of the building date back to the early 15th century, and mud and horsehair used to bulk out the plaster between the beams in each room is still visible. One, in the top floor attic rooms, even includes a set of ancient teeth – not human, in case you're wondering, and thought to have been provided by a butcher's shop across the road. Climb up here also for the outside terrace, which butts up against the churchyard of St Peter Hungate next door.

Address 9 Elm Hill, Norwich NR3 1HN, +44 (0)1603 331394, www.britonsarms.com | Getting there Purple Line buses to Tombland; 15-minute walk from the railway station | Hours Sun–Wed 9am–5.30pm, Thu–Sat 9am–9pm | Tip Across the street from the Britons Arms, The Monastery recalls a Benedictine order that was set up at 16 Elm Hill in 1864 by one Father Ignatius, a prominent 19th-century Catholic evangelist. Ignatius was a controversial character locally, and the monastery lasted just two years, having been attacked on a regular basis by anti-Catholic mobs.

17 Bure Valley Railway

Norfolk's longest narrow-gauge railway

Just eight miles north-east of Norwich, Wroxham is often known as the 'Gateway to the Broads', but when people refer to Wroxham it's actually its twin village of Hoveton they're talking about – whose centre is home to most of the commercial activity in this holiday centre for the Broads National Park. Hoveton is, however, also the gateway to the small town of Aylsham in the form of the dinky Bure Valley Railway, which lies just across the road from the regular main-line station of Wroxham & Hoveton.

The Bure Valley Railway is an old-fashioned mini (15in gauge) train line that runs from Hoveton to Aylsham, about nine miles to the north-west, taking in Coltishall, Buxton and Brampton along the way. The engines it uses are either steam- or diesel-powered, and the trip takes 45 minutes. The train itself is delightful, made up of several immaculately turned-out wooden carriages, and is a good and fairly painless way to see some proper Norfolk countryside on what is an easy day-trip from Norwich. If you don't want to take the train, you can also walk or cycle along the Bure Valley Path, which shadows the railway line – and the river – all the way to Aylsham.

You can just enjoy the journey there and back by train, or take the train in one direction and walk back in the other if you have the time and energy: there are plenty of good spots to stop for a picnic along the way and Coltishall has a couple of very good pubs for a spot of lunch, as does Aylsham itself.

Finally, kids of all ages (well, 18 and over) can sign up for one of their Steam Train Driver Day, on which it's possible to prepare and drive the locomotive; they also run afternoon tea trips and other seasonal events at Halloween and Christmas. Hoveton Station is also home to the marvellous Buffer Stop Books, which makes it a great place to browse while you are waiting for your train.

Address Belaugh Road, Hoveton, Norfolk NR12 8UU, +44 (0)1263 733858, www.bvrw.co.uk | Getting there Train to Wroxham & Hoveton | Hours BVR trains run several times daily Apr–Oct, the rest of the time they run during school holidays and at weekends; the station café is open 9am–4pm when trains are running. | Tip Aylsham is a very pleasant place to spend the day, maybe picking up a picnic lunch at Bread Source on the market square before heading out to nearby Blickling Hall.

18   Caistor St Edmund

Evocative ruins of East Anglia's Roman capital

A few miles south of Norwich, the village of Caistor St Edmund is mainly visited for the nearby site of Venta Icenorum – a Roman town that was the 'marketplace of the Iceni', the tribe that inhabited much of East Anglia during Roman times, of whom Boudicca is the most famous warrior. Settled after the Iceni revolt of A.D. 60, Venta was the largest Roman town and capital of the east of England for a time, growing from a small settlement in A.D. 70 to a much larger place in the late 3rd century, when the city walls were added.

There's nothing much to see now, but it's an evocative site none-theless – a large windswept field bordered on one side by the gently flowing river Tas, and surrounded by the denuded walls and towers of the Roman settlement. At one end, the church of St Edmund adds an extra splash of interest, an extremely ancient church dating back to the 1100s.

Caistor's walls make an ideal focal point for a stroll, punctuated by information boards detailing the nature of the settlement, and illustrating how it would have looked in its heyday. On the far side, the West Gate, by the river, was probably Venta's main entrance. The town was at its largest by the 4th century, when it would have had a population of around 2,000, most of whom would have been locals rather than Romans. Despite that, it would have been a wealthy, well-appointed sort of place, with an amphitheatre, baths, temples and forum. Discoveries by archaeologists have confirmed that the town was both an industrial and agricultural centre, at the heart of grazing and arable land, but also producing glass, ceramics and other products.

After the Romans left in the 5th century, Venta declined, eventually being abandoned in favour of Norwich around 200 years later, leaving the pristine site you see today (though one with sadly little in the way of remains).

Address Stoke Road, Caistor St Edmund, Norwich NR14 8QL | **Getting there** By car, 15–20-minute drive from the centre of Norwich, or take bus 40 or 41 | **Hours** 24 hours; free guided tours Sun 2.30pm May–Sep, and Wed 2.30pm Jul–Aug | **Tip** It's half a mile or so's stroll from the site to the next village of Stoke Holy Cross, whose excellent gastropub, The Wildebeest, is a nice place to round off your trip out of town. On a sunny day – and with a car – you might even drive for another five minutes to Shotesham Ford, which is a popular swimming spot off the main road just outside the village.

19__Carrow Road

Home to Norwich City FC

Formed in 1902, Norwich City are an important part of Norwich even among non-football fans – a plucky symbol of the city that traditionally yo-yos between the Championship and Premier League without really being at home in either. Known as The Canaries, their distinctive yellow and green kit marks them out among other big city clubs, as does their ownership, which is famously headed by TV and celebrity chef Delia Smith and her husband Michael Wynn-Jones.

Delia is the best-known supporter of a club that inspires real devotion in its fans (also united in their rivalry with nearby Ipswich Town). Formed by a group of teachers at the Criterion Café on White Lion Street (currently occupied by Moss Bros), and originally known as 'The Citizens', the club song – 'On the Ball City' – is said to be the oldest football chant in the world. The club first played at a ground on Newmarket Road before moving to 'The Nest', a disused chalk pit near the station (next door to the Rosary Cemetery), then to the current ground, Carrow Road, in 1935. The stadium has since then been completely redeveloped, and although a bit of a hotchpotch of styles the Barclay Stand is still named after the local man who paid for the roof in 1937. Overall, the feel is – like the club itself – family orientated and inclusive.

Tours take in the dressing rooms – including the deliberately downbeat away dressing room and the far more impressive home dressing room, complete with inspirational slogans, squad names and numbers and the dreaded ice bath. The trophy cabinet naturally gets a look-in, complete with pennants from City's famous 1993 European Cup run, while the directors' box gives a fabulous view over the 27,000-capacity stadium, including the notorious 'Snake Pit' in the corner and the pitch itself, the scene of Delia's famously rousing 'Let's be having you' speech in 2005.

Address Norwich City Football Club, Carrow Road, Norwich NR1 1JE, www.canaries.co.uk |
Getting there Less than a 10-minute walk from Norwich railway station | **Hours** Tours run
every day except the day before a home game, on a matchday or the day after a home game.
Call ahead to book a time. | **Tip** Norwich is a proper family club, right down to the catering,
with Delia's Canary Catering naturally taking care of all food and drink requirements in the
stadium. On a typical matchday they serve over 1,200 meals, many of which follow the TV
chef's recipes – even the sausage rolls are made to Delia's mum's recipe!

20 Cathedral of St John the Baptist

Norwich's Gothic Revival masterpiece

Begun in 1882 on the site of the old city gaol by George Gilbert Scott Jr, and finally completed almost three decades later by his brother, Norwich's Cathedral of St John the Baptist is one of the greatest examples of Gothic Revival ecclesiastical architecture in the country. Built as the plain old parish church of St John (funded by the famous Norfolk Catholic Howard family), it was only officially designated a cathedral in the 1970s, almost a decade after construction first began, as the titular church of the newly created Roman Catholic diocese of East Anglia – making Norwich one of the few UK cities to boast two cathedrals.

George Gilbert Scott Jr was in many ways continuing the work of his father, who was the 19th century's greatest exponent of the Gothic Revival. But his son also went his own way, converting to Catholicism and founding the exclusive clerical garments firm Watts & Co. The cathedral is his greatest building, but even before starting it, he is said to have suffered mental health problems, and was eventually hospitalised by his brother, who took over his practice and construction of the church, which was finished in 1910: as a result, the nave is by the elder of the two brothers, the choir by both.

St John is now the second-largest Catholic cathedral in the country, and an impressive, classically Victorian structure right by the city's inner ring road. Overall, it's a very welcoming place, always open to visitors, with a shop and busy café that opens out onto the cathedral gardens. Simple in style yet ambitious in scope, its elegantly pointed arches flank a nave that is some 49 metres long, with nine bays topped by blind galleries, and simple ribbed vaulting. Either side, the fabulous stained glass windows are contemporary with the church, and wonderful examples of Victorian style.

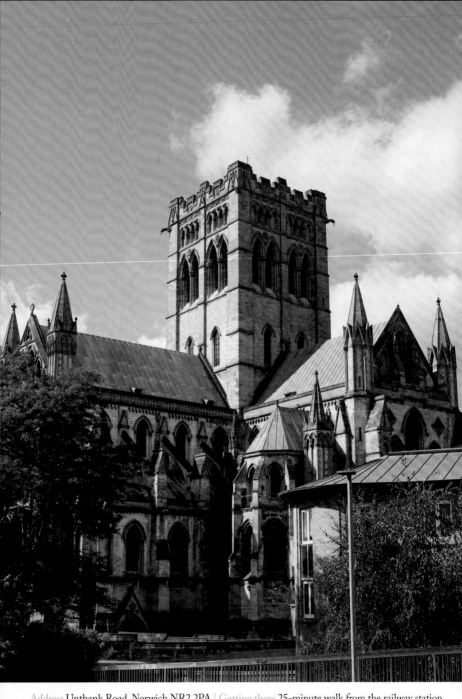

Address Unthank Road, Norwich NR2 2PA | Getting there 25-minute walk from the railway station, or you can take bus 21 or 22 | Hours Daily 7.30am–7.30pm | Tip Tours of the cathedral tower give predictably fabulous views over the city – and indeed over the interior of the church on the way.

21 _ Cathedral Precincts
Delightful grounds to supplement a cathedral visit

Norwich Cathedral is something special, and it's hard to do justice to it in a single chapter, let alone its precincts, which occupy an 85-acre site in the centre of the city. Whatever you do, don't visit the cathedral without exploring its historic surroundings, which form a unique complex right in the heart of Norwich that was formerly the grounds of a Benedictine priory, founded here in the late 11th century – much of which was spared demolition during the dissolution. Wandering through these grounds is a delight, particularly on a sunny day, and there's even a good café shoe-horned into the old monks' refectory that's handy for a restorative, post-stroll cuppa.

Originally there would have been a wall around the complex, with four gates providing access from the street – Bishopgate and Water Gate (at Pulls Ferry), and St Ethelberts and Erpingham Gate on the city centre side. St Ethelberts dates from 1316, while the grander Erpingham Gate is a century or so older, and both give access to the wide rectangle of Upper Close, framed by Georgian houses behind you and with the cathedral in front, beyond which Norwich School is tucked into the corner and incorporates the original 11th century Bishop's Palace.

Cutting through from the Upper Close to the Lower Close, on the left you pass the Chapter Office, originally a medieval infirmary, with the herb garden of the cathedral planted in front. Beyond here, the street opens out on to the oval of Lower Close, lined with medieval dwellings, including the step-gabled Deanery on your left and a former bakehouse and brewhouse at the far end. From here you can take one of several routes – left off the square down what looks and feels like a medieval street, from where a path leads through the playing fields of Norwich School to Bishopgate and the Great Hospital, or right, down to the river on Ferry Lane.

Address Norwich NR1 4DH | **Getting there** You can enter the cathedral precincts from several different places: the most usual is from Tombland through the Upper Close, but you can also enter from Bishopgate and Pull's Ferry, by the river, and finally from Recorder Road (see below). | **Hours** Always open | **Tip** A third path from Lower Close branches off Ferry Lane and leads out of the cathedral precincts to Recorder Road, and the dinky James Stuart Garden, with its fancy gatehouse. This was designed by Edward Boardman in 1922 (also responsible for the nearby almshouses – see ch. 79) and named after the very popular Liberal MP husband of Laura Colman.

22 Cinema City

Norwich's best cinema and a historic site

Yet another cultural venue housed in one of Norwich's many historic buildings, Cinema City is loved not just by local culture vultures, but also plenty of people who like to meet and have a drink or bite to eat in its convivial bar and café. It's part of the nationwide 'Picture House' chain, so is mostly a place to see mainstream movies, but it also screens its share of arthouse flicks, along with hosting one-off events and showings of old favourites, retrospectives, and even the odd premiere. There are three screens, and the cinema celebrated no less than 40 years on this site in 2018, when it also made long-time Norfolk resident John Hurt one of its patrons.

Cinema City is a historic site too. Part of the building occupies the Suckling House, a Grade I listed, mainly 16th-century building that was the home of one Robert Suckling, who was mayor of Norwich in the 1570s and 1580s – although parts of the building date back to the 14th century (much like Strangers Hall just down the road – see ch. 95). It was restored by Jeremiah Colman's daughter Ethel (who just happened to be the UK's first female Lord Mayor) in 1923. She also added the Stuart Hall extension to the St Andrew's Hill side of the building: named after Ethel's late sister, Laura Stuart, this was designed by the prolific and popular Norwich architect Edward Boardman (see ch. 79). In 1925, Ethel bequeathed Suckling House in its entirety to the City of Norwich, to be used for 'the advancement of education in its widest and most comprehensive sense'.

Most of the house itself, including Stuart Hall, is now mainly occupied by the cinema's café and restaurant. The Great Hall forms the bar, and a series of rooms with 14th-century vaulted ceilings, arches and panels make up the restaurant space, along with a pleasant courtyard – well worth a visit, regardless of whether you're here to see a movie.

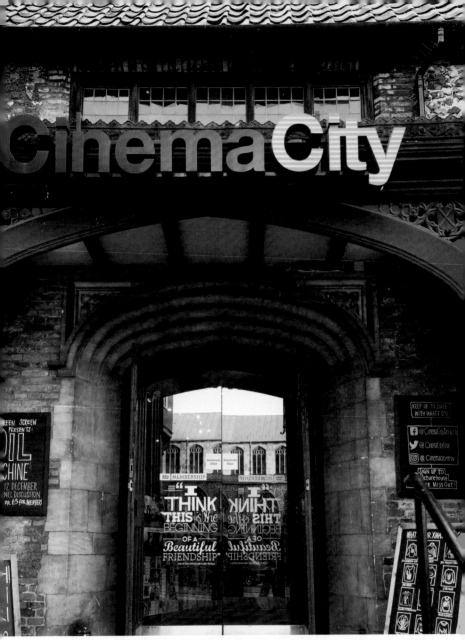

Address St Andrew's Street, Norwich NR2 4AD, www.picturehouses.com/cinema/cinema-city-picturehouse | **Getting there** Short walk from Market Place and Castle Meadow buses | **Hours** Films shown daily 10am–11pm; bar-restaurant open Mon–Sat 10am–11pm, Sun 10am–9pm | **Tip** If you're lucky enough to gain entry, it's worth a peek into the church of St Andrew's next door, home to the Suckling Chapel and the tombs of Robert and John Suckling and their wives, commemorated by life-sized prone effigies clad in armour.

23 — City Hall

The very model of municipal modernism

One of Norwich's most monumental buildings, City Hall is municipal modernism at its most magnificent, taking up almost the entire west side of the city's Market Place, with officially the longest balcony in the country and a clock tower that rises to just over 56 metres. The architectural historian Nikolaus Pevsner called it the 'foremost English building between the wars', and he wasn't far wrong, although even now it has almost as many detractors as admirers. It's one of the so-called 'Norwich 12' – a dozen buildings in the city designated of special architectural significance.

A replacement for a decrepit collection of buildings that previously housed the city council, City Hall was finished in 1938, its design the winner of a competition held earlier in the decade. The strident lions on the steps proclaim the building as Norwich HQ, along with the bronze doors, whose panel reliefs tell the story of Norwich's industries through the ages – there's a key to what's what here in the foyer, where another panel details the names of the city's mayors since 1403, opposite a Lutyens-designed WWI roll of honour. Lutyens also designed the war memorial directly in front of City Hall.

Those lucky enough to get upstairs can treat themselves to a peek at the Council Chamber, which fills by far the largest part of the L-shaped building, and a corridor devoted to all sorts of Norwich-related material – gifts from its twin cities (Rouen, Koblenz, Novi Sad), portraits of 18th- and 19th-century mayors, and a signed Norwich City shirt from their last promotion to the Premier League, when the team appeared on the balcony outside. Hitler was apparently so impressed with the building, and the tantalising thought of goose-stepping up and down the long balcony, that he ordered his bombers to leave it intact, which explains why it remains such a fine example of an art deco-style building.

Address St Peter's Street, Norwich NR2 1NH | Getting there Lots of buses stop nearby; 10-minute walk from the railway station | Hours Mon–Fri 9am–5pm | Tip Norfolk County Council occupies another 20th-century landmark building on the edge of town – County Hall – a slab-like structure designed by the modernist architect Reginald Uren in the late 1960s and built on land acquired from the Colman mustard dynasty.

24 City Walls

Discovering the walls of the medieval city

Travelling around Norwich, you are always aware that it was a walled settlement; there are remnants of the city's once formidable walls everywhere, tumbledown flint monoliths originally built in the late 13th and early 14th centuries. They didn't encircle the city, but were positioned at its north, south and west sides, with the eastern side's security provided by the river, with the only entry across the river at Bishopgate. For centuries, these walls and the river formed the boundary of the city, with little built outside them until the late 18th century.

The best-preserved stretch of city wall is the hardest to find – at the far end of King Street and Rouen Road, near Carrow Road football ground, where a stepped path leads up the hill just across Koblenz Avenue. The path forks around a hollow tower and leads to the so-called Black Tower, which sits in a strategic position on a ridge above Carrow Hill, and is one of the city's largest remaining defensive towers. Ten metres across, the tower was built as a strategic lookout, surveying land to the south, but it was also used to house plague victims during the Black Death. From here, the wall runs in both directions, one path tracking the wall around the tower and down the hill, another following the inside of a well-preserved stretch of wall, where you can see arrow slits and windows, as well as holes made for the scaffolding when the walls were built.

There's another short stretch of wall at the end of nearby Ber Street, where there was another entry point to the city, while back towards the football ground are the remains of freestanding riverside towers, known as the Boom Towers, which were linked by a chain and used to stop – and tax – goods entering the city. Finally, there's another short stretch of city wall on Chapelfield Road from St Stephen's roundabout up to Chapelfield Gardens.

Address 32 Carrow Hill, Norwich NR1 2BH | Getting there The path up to the Black Tower and Carrow Hill is a 3-minute walk from Carrow Road football stadium; 10-minute walk from the railway station | Hours Always open | Tip At the end of your exploration, take the weight off your feet in Chapelfield Gardens, an oasis of green space next to the Chantry Place shopping centre. Fringed on one side by a row of elegant Georgian houses, and on the other by the city walls, there's a kids' playground, a café and a bandstand, although sadly it no longer has its once magnificent Pagoda, designed in 1876 by Thomas Jeckyll.

25 __ Colegate

Main Street of 'Norwich Over the Water'

One of Norwich's most interesting historical areas lies across the river Wensum to the south of the original city walls, and has been known for centuries as 'Norwich Over the Water' or 'Ultra Aquam' in medieval times. Thought to be the location of Norwich's original Anglo-Saxon settlement, it was originally known as Westwic. With easy access to the river, it was an area of commerce, home to the textile industry since the days of The Strangers (see ch. 95), many of whom settled in the area, and later the city's shoe industry, clustered around two main arteries of Magdalen Street and Colegate.

Colegate stretches from Magdalen Street to the former industrial district of Coslany in the west, and remains one of the city's most historically significant thoroughfares, anchored at each end by medieval churches: St Clement, on the corner of Magdalen Street, and St Michael Coslany at its western end. The former was one of the first churches built here during medieval times, but has been redundant since the 1960s, while the latter is a beautiful 15th-century structure that is also sadly redundant; in fact only one of Colegate's churches still functions: St George (see ch. 88), along with two non-denominational chapels (see ch. 65 & 66).

In between, the 16th-century timbered house of wealthy wool merchant Henry Bacon is said to have hosted talks during Kett's rebellion. Opposite, Amelia Opie (see ch. 3) lived in a house that once stood on the site of the old Shoe Factory, formerly known as the Norvic works. Norwich was once home to around 30 shoe factories, but this one is perhaps its most handsome, built in 1876 by Edward Boardman (see ch. 79), when the area was a mixture of industrial buildings and slum housing. The building is now home to a school, while a second nearby factory – St Mary's Works, just off Duke Street – is being revamped as a space for arts and artists.

Address Colegate, Norwich NR3 | **Getting there** The nicest way to get to 'Norwich Over the Water' is simply to walk across the river from St Andrew's Street by way of Blackfriars Bridge, and stroll up St Georges Street to Colegate. | **Hours** Always accessible | **Tip** Colegate is close to some good places to eat and drink, not least the Norwich Playhouse by the river, whose legendary bar is one of the city centre's best places for a drink. There's also the cosy and long-established Last Wine Bar, and the funky Asian-inspired XO Kitchen, between Colegate and the river.

26 __ Delia's

One of Norwich's best foodie experiences

Well insulated from the roar of the crowd and, indeed, pretty much everything else, there's nothing quite as soothing as a visit to Delia's – the fine dining restaurant of the nation's favourite TV chef, Delia Smith. The establishment is housed slightly incongruously in the Regency Stand at Carrow Road, home of Norwich City FC, which the chef owns with her husband Michael Wynn-Jones. Both are long-term fans and season-ticket holders, and they became majority owners of the club in 1996.

Delia Smith was arguably the UK's first celebrity chef, not only regularly appearing on TV from the 1970s until the early 2000s, but also racking up record sales of her numerous cookbooks (she also famously baked the cake that appears on the cover of the 1969 Rolling Stones album Let it Bleed!). Delia's homely, unpretentious style made her a huge favourite in households across Britain, and although eventually overtaken by edgier rivals, Delia remains arguably better-known, more successful and more highly regarded than any of the gastronomic gurus who succeeded her. She is also the football club's most famous supporter by some margin. The associated restaurant is the flagship outlet of her Canary Catering group, which runs all the catering in the stadium, and hosts events and regular food and wine workshops.

The restaurant is one of Norwich's biggest foodie treats on a Friday or Saturday night. It's the sort of place where coats are taken, greetings profuse, and waiters glide silently past as you perch on a bar stool sampling a canapé, while browsing a menu full of impeccably presented seasonal dishes. You don't even have to be spectacularly flush to enjoy it: the three-course menu goes for under £50, and the wine selections are deliberately affordable. As with her cookery books, Delia shows us that running a quality restaurant can make culinary delights accessible to all.

Address Carrow Road Stadium, Norwich NR1 1JE, +44 (0)1603 218705,
www.deliascanarycatering.co.uk | Getting there 10-minute walk from the railway station |
Hours Fri & Sat 6–11pm | Tip An alternative to the fine dining at Delia's is Yellows,
on the ground floor of the same stand, which is open much longer hours and serves cheaper
and simpler food, which nonetheless carries Delia's unmistakable mark of quality.

27 Dragon Hall

Medieval hall now National Centre for Writing

Running from Rose Lane to the river, King Street is one of Norwich's most historic thoroughfares, though it's now flanked by undistinguished new developments, waste ground and a mix of buildings from various eras. But during the Middle Ages it was a riverside district at the heart of industrial Norwich, famous among other things for no fewer than 58 pubs – only one of which survives: the appropriately named 'Last Pub Standing'.

Dragon Hall is the most notable of the historic structures, home to perhaps the most intact example of a medieval merchant's trading hall that you'll ever see. Although the oldest part of the building dates back to 1330, and was a domestic dwelling, this main hall was added in the mid-15th century by the then owner, Robert Topps, as a space for trading textiles, wines and spices, which were unloaded on the nearby riverfront. Shortly after Topps' death in 1467 it was turned into a series of private dwellings, which it remained until the slum clearances of the early 20th century.

The beamed hall Topps built to trade his wares is amazing, with an original crown post roof made with the wood of 1,000 oak trees, and decorated with wrought iron supports with roaring dragons – though sadly only one of these remains. At 26 metres long, it's full of fascinating detail: take a look at the so-called 'witches' marks' on the beams – black scorch marks made in the middle ages to ward off evil spirits. These are a nice counterpoint to the fragments of wallpaper clinging to the beams, remnants of the building's later conversion to flats.

Extended in the 1980s, Dragon Hall is now home to the National Centre for Writing, which celebrates creative writing in all its forms and works with local schools, running workshops, events and monthly social get-togethers. It's also home to Brewer's Cottage, a (supposedly haunted) residence for writers and poets.

Address 115-123 King Street, Norwich NR1 1QE, www.nationalcentreforwriting.org.uk/dragon-hall | Getting there Blue Line buses 25 and 26 pass nearby; 15-minute walk from the railway station | Hours Free tours every second Monday of the month | Tip King Street has several historic houses, the most important of which besides Dragon Hall is probably Music House at 167-169, which dates back to the 12th century and is reckoned to be the oldest dwelling house in the city.

28 Eaton Park

Everything an urban park should be

Just the other side of Norwich's inner ring road, and a hop, skip and a jump from its so-called Golden Triangle (see ch. 106), Eaton Park is probably the city centre's most enjoyable park. The land was purchased by the city council at the turn of the 20th century, with its 80 or so acres used as a practice ground for trench warfare, before being laid out as a public park in the 1920s by military man Arnold Edward Sandys-Winsch. He was Norwich's parks superintendent after World War I, and responsible for endowing the city with many other parks, including nearby Waterloo Park, which boasts one of the longest herbaceous borders in the UK. Sandys-Winsch's plan for Eaton Park provided it with a grand array of buildings and pavilions as part of a Depression-era work scheme, although later the war encroached again, when the pavilion's colonnades were set aside to house air raid casualties.

Officially opened by the Prince of Wales in 1928, Eaton Park remains very popular, attracting a wide variety of people: elderly strollers and dog-walkers, skateboarding teens, sports enthusiasts who use its football pitches and tennis courts, and families with young kids visiting to ride on the miniature railway. There's also an expansive model yachting pond, next to which there are benches dedicated to both Sandys-Winsch and the men who built the park, along with an 18-hole pitch-and-putt course that fills a more wooded, bucolic enclave on the northern side of the park.

There's an elegant colonnaded circular pavilion, Grade II listed and centred on a columned bandstand, which forms a natural centre for the park's activities. It's home to an excellent dog-friendly café, whose tables spread into the arches outside. Overall, the vibe is one of gentle activity and a community at rest and relaxation – everything, in fact, that an urban park should be.

Address Norwich NR14 7AU | Getting there Blue Line bus 25 passes by the park | Hours 24 hours; café open daily 10am–4pm | Tip A short walk north-east from Eaton Park, across Christchurch Road, the much smaller Heigham Park was also laid out by Sandys-Winsch.

29 _ Edith Cavell Memorial

'Patriotism is not enough'

Born in the suburb of Swardeston to the south of Norwich in 1865, local heroine Edith Cavell is commemorated all over the city, and beyond – perhaps the most famous memorial to her stands at the bottom of St Martin's Lane, just off Trafalgar Square in London. Her principal marker, however, stands outside the gates of Norwich cathedral on Tombland: a head-and-shoulders statue of the World War I nurse and martyr by Henry Pegram, unveiled in 1918.

It's no surprise that we still remember Cavell. She travelled regularly between Norwich and Belgium during the early years of the 20th century, and founded the country's first training school for nurses in Brussels. After Belgium was invaded by Germany in 1914, she based herself there, caring for both Allied and German casualties. She also secretly helped Allied soldiers escape back to Britain – something forbidden on penalty of death by the German occupiers. In all, she is said to have helped some 200 soldiers escape, before being discovered. As a result, she spent two months in solitary confinement before being executed by firing squad on 12 October, 1915.

The execution of such a prominent humanitarian was widely condemned, and Cavell was immediately declared a national hero. Her body was repatriated to England after the war and given a state funeral in Westminster Abbey. The memorial statue is more modest than its London equivalent, though still rather stirring, a foot soldier clasping a wreath below her proud and resolute gaze. Her grave, a short walk away, just outside one of the south-eastern doors of the cathedral, is an altogether more moving affair: a simple headstone bearing the words that have resonated most down the years – 'In the light of God and eternity I have realised that patriotism is not enough, I must have no hatred or bitterness towards anyone' – and perhaps best summarise her motivations.

Address Tombland, Norwich NR3 1RF | Getting there Purple Line buses to Tombland; 10–15-minute walk from the railway station | Hours Always accessible | Tip If you peek through the 15th-century Erpingham Gate into the cathedral close you'll see a statue to another Norfolk-born national hero, Admiral Lord Nelson, who attended Norwich School, opposite. Depicted with telescope and cannon, the memorial was daubed with graffiti as part of a Black Lives Matter protest in 2020.

30 — Elizabeth Fry

Famous social reformer and feminist

Born into the wealthy Gurney banking family in 1780, Elizabeth Fry could be considered the most famous and influential woman to be born in Norwich – certainly one of the most important social reformers of the 19th century. One of 12 children, she is commemorated by a plaque in an alleyway at 33 Magdalen Street, where she was born at Gurney House – now a private residence. Elizabeth didn't live in the city centre for very long, moving to Earlham Hall (now part of the University of East Anglia) at the age of six. A practising Quaker, she married her husband Joseph Fry at the Old Meeting House on Upper Goat Lane in 1800, and shortly after began to make her name protesting about the conditions that women in particular endured at prisons such as London's Newgate.

Fry worked tirelessly to improve the lot of women and the poor, and regularly visited female offenders, taking them clothes and food, and often reading to them from the Bible. In 1817, she set up the Association for the Improvement of Female Prisoners, which lobbied Parliament to reform prisons – which they eventually did, starting with the Gaols Act of 1823. She also campaigned for better conditions for convicts transported to Australia, and also the revolutionary idea that prisons should be more about rehabilitation than punishment. She also highlighted the plight of the poor in Victorian England, especially London, setting up homeless shelters, campaigned against slavery, and promoted religious tolerance.

Fry travelled widely and spent more of her life in London and Kent than in Norwich, resulting in memorials to her all over the country – in East Ham and Ramsgate, where she lived, and even in the Old Bailey and at Wormwood Scrubs (in Canada they celebrate 'Elizabeth Fry Week' every year!), and the eponymous charity continues her work, helping women find housing and opportunities after leaving prison.

Address Gurney Court, 33 Magdalen Street, Norwich NR3 1LQ | Getting there Several buses go down Magdalen Street; 15–20-minute walk from the railway station | Hours Always open | Tip The plaque next to Elizabeth's at Gurney Court is a memorial to another trailblazing woman, Harriet Martineau, who was born in the same house, in 1802. A strict Unitarian who worshipped at the nearby Octagon Chapel, she is considered one of the first real feminists.

ELIZABETH FRY
1780 – 1845
Founded an Association for improving the conditions of Female Prisoners in Newgate 1817, and her efforts resulted in a complete change of prison management in this and other Countries.

Born at Gurney House
in the adjacent Court.

31 Elm Hill

The city's most photographed street?

Elm Hill is arguably the most famous street in Norwich, and it's easy to see why – it's one of the oldest and best-preserved old lanes in the city centre, its cobbles curving elegantly down the hill flanked by an assortment of picturesque, leaning medieval houses. Unsurprisingly, this is Norwich's most photographed street, and was highly regarded even a hundred years ago, when J. B. Priestley exclaimed that its 'bowed and twisted fronts' were home to 'an assortment of misers, mad spinsters, saintly clergymen, eccentric comic clerks, and lunatic sextons'. All the world, then!

At the top of Elm Hill there's a triangular square centred on a plane tree, planted on the spot that used to be home to the eponymous elm tree. There are a number of shops, and although it isn't the sort of street you visit to buy groceries, it's not as pretentious as might be expected. It's home to a couple of stores selling antiques and collectables, a clutch of cafés (including the venerable Britons Arms at the top – see ch. 16) and the occasional second-hand book shop.

Wright's Court, down a passageway at number 43, is one of the few remaining enclosed courtyards that were once a feature of the city, while halfway down on the left, the street's most historic building – apart from the Britons Arms – is the Strangers Club. Built in the early 16th century by the mayor of the city at the time, Augustine Steward, the site was previously occupied by the Pastons, one of Norfolk's richest and most influential families during the 15th century, and famous for the 'Paston Letters' – a unique and revealing collection of correspondence made during the Wars of the Roses. As for the Strangers Club, it's probably Norwich's most exclusive private members' club, set up in 1927 by six local bigwigs to entertain guests and visitors to the city and still open to gentlemen only (though female partners are allowed in!).

Address Elm Hill, Norwich NR3 1HG | Getting there Purple Line buses to Tombland; 15-minute walk from the railway station | Hours Always accessible | Tip As you might expect, the cobbles of Elm Hill are a favourite with film producers looking for authentically ancient locations, and the street has featured in a number of movies over the years, from the 2007 film *Stardust* to the more recent Netflix Christmas flick *Jingle Jangle*, starring Hugh Bonneville.

32 Fairhaven Water Garden

A gorgeous microcosm of the Broads

If you want a taster of the Broads, there's no better place than Fairhaven Water Gardens, just outside the village of South Walsham. A dozen miles from the city, this provides an easy (land- and wheelchair-accessible) glimpse of the swampy wilderness that makes up so much of the region. The gardens cover around 130 acres from the village down to South Walsham Broad, and came into the Fairhaven family in a state of ruin just after World War II. It was renovated by the second Lord Fairhaven, one Major Henry Broughton, who left it to a trust on his death in 1973, since when the gardens have been open to the public. It's a really special place, and given the lure of these surroundings, it's perhaps no surprise that there have been only two people in charge of the gardens since they opened in the 1970s.

The current custodian, Louise Rout, is passionate about Fairhaven, and no wonder: its woodland, dykes and creeks, crossed by wooden bridges and cut through with shady paths, form a uniquely lovely spot. Whatever the time of year, there's always something to see. There's an oak tree that's almost 1,000 years old, a fish pond that was mentioned in the Domesday Book, and any number of flowering plants and shrubs – rhododendrons, camellias and literally thousands of candelabra primula that flower every May and June.

Organically managed, the gardens lead down to the estate's private section of South Walsham Broad, where you can sometimes see an otter or two, take a boat trip – either a gentle spin round the Broad or to nearby St Benet's Abbey and back – or just sit and watch the water. There are also special trails for kids, and canoe trips, paddle-boarding and wild swimming sessions. There's a decent café serving sandwiches, hot food and excellent scones, and a healthy selection of plants for sale just outside the shop. Overall, it's a relaxing family treat – worth visiting at any time of year.

Address School Road, South Walsham, Norwich NR13 6DZ, +44 (0)1603 270449, www.fairhavengarden.co.uk | Getting there By car, a 20-minute drive from central Norwich | Hours Daily from 9am; check website for current information on closing times | Tip The next-door village of Ranworth is home to another iconic Broads location, St Helen's Church, known as the 'Cathedral of the Broads'. Climbing its tower gives spectacular birds-eye views over its unique, watery landscape.

33 Fairhurst Gallery

Historic gallery and workshop

Easy to miss on Bedford Street, Fairhurst Gallery is located in the heart of the Norwich Lanes: a set of narrow streets and alleys that's home to the city's independent shops and restaurants, and one of Norwich's most historic districts. Indeed, the gallery occupies two historic buildings located next door to each other, separated by an ancient alley. Formerly the Cat Trap jazz club, it's always been a funky sort of place, and is now the workspace of husband-and-wife team Dulcie and Tom Humphrey, who between them run one of Norwich city centre's best art galleries and picture framing workshops.

The Fairhurst Gallery actually pre-dates the Humphreys by a few decades. The original business was located on Elm Hill, and run by local artist, dealer and ex-soldier Joe Fairhurst. Fairhurst not only showcased his own still-life works and landscapes, but also those of prominent East Anglian artists such as Alfred Munnings and Edward Seago. Fairhurst's son Timothy – nicknamed 'Tiz' – later took over the business, establishing a framing workshop and moving to the current premises on Bedford Street, before eventually passing the business on to Tom and Dulcie in 2013.

The gallery – run by Dulcie – hosts regular exhibitions, often but not exclusively featuring local Norwich and Norfolk artists. The artists represented over the years include the Great Yarmouth painter Bruer Tidman, Broads-based artist Alex Egan, and Norfolk artists such as Kate O'Grady, Harry Cory Wright and Nigel Moody. Tom, meanwhile, works in the workshop located in the 18th-century building next door. This is a former shoe factory that's now devoted to framing, gilding and restoration. It's a large space, which is just as well, as customers include Norwich Cathedral, the Castle, and even the Sainsbury Centre – although regular mortals are also welcome to bring their pictures here too!

Address 17 Bedford Street, Norwich NR2 1AR, +44 (0)1603 614214, www.fairhurstgallery.co.uk | Getting there 15-minute walk from the railway station or a couple of minutes from the bus stops on Castle Meadow | Hours Tue–Sat 9.30am–5.30pm | Tip Other Norwich art galleries include the Anteros Arts Foundation, housed in a historic Tudor building on Fye Bridge Street, and the artist-founded and -run Outpost Gallery on Wensum Street, next door to St Simon and St Jude's church.

34 The Fat Cat
A fine pub and brewery

Born in Norwich, Colin Keatley ran away with his father to run a pub in London when he was 15, and has been in the trade ever since. He took on his own pub aged just 21, and returned to Norwich in the early 1980s, when he ran the White Lion on Oak Street. He then established the Fat Cat in 1991 with his wife Marjie, when they bought the almost derelict New Inn, just off the Dereham Road.

Colin's love of pubs and good beer is immediately evident as you step through the door of The Fat Cat. Colin was determined to create the sort of no-frills boozer he likes himself, serving excellent beer in a traditional environment, with little in the way of food and certainly no fruit machines or loud music – just the hum of local people connecting and enjoying themselves. It's a simple but effective formula, and The Fat Cat was pretty much a success from the outset. Indeed, the pub has won CAMRA's national 'Pub of the Year' award three times, as well being named 'Beer Pub of the Year' 11 times in the annual Good Pub Guide.

Colin is still often in the pub, serving and engaging with his regulars, alongside his son, Will. The Fat Cat's range of beers does vary, but usually features one or two local brews, including the Fat Cat's own ales. These are brewed at their brewery on Lawson Road, which is also home to their very popular Brewery Tap. Situated in increasingly trendy NR3, this not only serves great, beer-friendly food, but also hosts bands and other events, and even has its own running and cycling clubs. The only food available in the original Fat Cat are the Lincolnshire pork pies that Colin gets delivered every week, served with lashings of mustard. You're welcome to order a takeaway and consume it at your table, though, especially if it's from Harry's Soul Station, located just around the corner – and whose burgers, toasties and soulfood come highly recommended by Colin and Will!

Address 49 West End Street, Norwich NR2 4NA, +44 (0)7807 579517, www.fatcatpub.co.uk | Getting there Red Line buses 23 and 24 follow Dereham Road | Hours Sun–Wed noon–10pm, Thu–Sat noon–11pm | Tip Get the full set of Fat Cats by trying the third and final Norwich Fat Cat, The Fat Cat & Canary on Thorpe Road, which repeats much the same formula as the Brewery Tap – great beer and a friendly local vibe, food you are welcome to eat from nearby takeaways plus DJs and live music.

35 Forncett Steam Museum

One man's tribute to the Industrial Revolution

Buried deep in the lanes and by-roads a few miles south of Norwich, the Forncett Industrial Steam Museum is a little gem well worth travelling out of the city for. The almost single-handed creation of one man – retired anaesthetist Rowan Francis, who lives next door – it is basically a unique insight into the machinery that powered Britain's industrial revolution, initially saved from the scrap heap by Rowan and a handful of like-minded individuals who could not bear to see them lost forever. Then, as Rowan says himself, 'like most hobbies, it just mushroomed'.

The museum has been open since 1982, but Rowan started collecting long before that, inspired by his father, who built a miniature steam railway in his back garden before moving on to create the Wells & Walsingham Light Railway in North Norfolk – still running to this day. Rowan not only shared his father's passion for steam, he could see that the engines that had powered British industry were gradually being replaced and not preserved; too heavy and cumbersome to move, they were broken up and disposed of instead.

Desperate to salvage these remnants of Britain's industrial past, Rowan found ways of rescuing these beasts that would have defeated lesser men – indeed the most incredible thing about this museum is that these engines are here at all. Not only did Rowan have to beg, steal and borrow to get them dismantled and moved, he then had to build concrete floors to accommodate them, reassemble them bit by bit, and literally build the museum building around them once they were in place. Rowan's remarkable story is told in a video, after which you can view these magnificent pieces of kit for yourself – from a Lincolnshire maltings engine to a massive pump engine from Dover, a monster that took over 20 years to reassemble, and even one of the engines that was once used to open Tower Bridge.

Address Low Road, Forncett St Mary, Norwich NR16 1JJ, +44 (0)1508 488277, www.forncettsteammuseum.co.uk | **Getting there** By car, around half an hour's drive from central Norwich – no public transport available | **Hours** Wed & Sun 10am–4pm; May–Oct first Sun of the month and Father's Day 10am–5pm | **Tip** Visit on the first Sunday of the month to see the engines in action, powered up with steam provided by a dramatically riveted boiler procured from Norwich prison!

36__The Forum

Perfect place to meet someone, any time of day

The Forum dominates the south-western corner of Norwich's market square with an impressive sense of presence. Built to be almost the epitome of civic pride, its glass frontage cleverly reflects all of the surrounding buildings, especially the church of St Peter Mancroft directly opposite (see ch. 94). Both literally and metaphorically, it encapsulates the essence of the city.

The Forum is certainly a daring piece of post-war architecture. Designed by the Michael Hopkins architectural firm and part funded by the Millennium Commission, it's a deliberately inclusive building – basically a horseshoe-shaped courtyard with a roof that forms a large atrium surrounded by balconies. Built on the site of the medieval city's French Quarter, which was established after the Norman Conquest in the 1070s, The Forum opened in 2002, having been built on the site of the previous Norwich Central Library, which was destroyed by fire in 1994. Made up of over 1,200 individual panes of glass, it is estimated to see just under two million visitors every year.

The Forum houses the BBC East TV and radio studios, the city's main public library and the Norfolk Heritage Centre, which includes ancient maps of the county, a 13th-century illuminated manuscript (the 'Norwich Apocalypse') and the first book ever printed in Norwich, in 1568. There are also special collections such as the Norfolk City Library (established in 1608), the personal library of Jeremiah Colman, and the American Library, which in part commemorates the 2nd Airborne Division, which was based here during World War II. Sadly, The Forum no longer houses the city's tourist information office, but it does act as one of the city's major large event spaces, its main hall always abuzz with some gathering or activity. Given its location and prominence, The Forum is the perfect place to meet someone, any time of day.

Address Bethel Street, Millennium Plain, Norwich NR2 1BH | **Getting there** Lots of buses stop nearby; 10-minute walk from the railway station | **Hours** Mon–Sat 8am–11pm, Sun 8.30am–11pm; Norfolk Heritage Centre open Mon–Fri 10am–7pm & Sat 9am–5pm | **Tip** The Forum is home to a popular café – Marzano – on its ground floor, with a branch of Pizza Express upstairs.

37 The Garnet

Terrific and unique city centre pub

It's been a watering hole since the mid-19th century, trading as The Sir Garnet Wolseley, right on the edge of the market place, so it's unsurprising that this venerable old pub is so well known and beloved of Norwich natives that it's adopted the much easier soubriquet of 'The Garnet'. It's still a pub, and still respectfully occupies what is a beautiful and unique old building, but one that's been catapulted into the 21st century by its energetic owner, Lauren Gregory.

The Garnet was originally known as the 'Baron of Beef', but changed its name in commemoration of one of Victorian England's most revered generals, who served in various colonial campaigns in Africa and elsewhere. He developed such a reputation for thoroughness that the phrase 'Everything's all Sir Garnet' was coined to describe any situation that's well organised and in order. Everything's certainly 'all Sir Garnet' at what is by any standards a terrific city centre pub. It's a unique place, with lots of nooks and crannies and several floors reached by a rickety staircase – the upper ones enjoying plum views over Norwich's market place.

A native of Great Yarmouth, Lauren worked as a model in London for a while, but returned to Norfolk and made a real impact on the Norwich pub scene – first with the iconic Birdcage on Pottergate, then The Garnet. The latter attracts a real mix of clientele, including young devotees in the evening, casual drinkers, and shoppers from the market. The pub serves decent beer and a terrific range of wines, which you can also buy (along with beers and whiskies) at off-licence prices. The Garnet doesn't serve food, but runs pop-ups with local restaurants a couple of times a week. And as long as you buy a drink you can always get something from the market and eat it at your table. Entertainment is provided by the occasional DJ, perhaps with a bit of dancing on the terrace outside in summer!

Address 36 Market Place, Norwich NR2 1RD, +44 (0)1603 615892, www.thegarnet.co.uk |
Getting there Lots of buses stop nearby; 10-minute walk from the railway station | Hours
Mon–Thu noon–11pm, Fri & Sat noon–midnight, Sun noon–6.30pm | Tip The Garnet
brand continues in the shop next door, which sells cool yet functional homewares, clothes and
locally-made crafts and other items, along with tea, coffee and cakes.

38 __ George Skipper's Grave

Norwich's Gaudi leaves indelible mark on the city

Born in nearby Dereham, George Skipper is little known outside Norfolk, but in the late 19th and early 20th century he was the most sought-after architect of his day in these parts. This was particularly the case in Norwich, and he was responsible for many of the buildings of that era that are still standing today, as well as many others throughout East Anglia – though his grave, in Earlham Cemetery, is a surprisingly simple affair.

Probably the most visited of Skipper's buildings is the Royal Arcade (see ch. 78), which Skipper adapted from a hotel in 1899, but if you can you should also visit the reception of the uncompromisingly grand office headquarters he built for the Norwich Union insurance company on Surrey Street (see ch. 99). Not only was Skipper a decorative architect, he was also very much a man of his time, an architectural magpie who incorporated all sorts of styles from different eras into this work – swirls and cartouches, columns and plinths, recesses and bay windows: everything has a place in his vision.

Skipper was also extraordinarily prolific, and left his mark right across the city centre. There are two notable Skipper buildings located next to each other on Red Lion Street – one, the florid Commercial Chambers, inspired John Betjeman to describe Skipper as '…remarkable and original. He is to Norwich what Gaudi was to Barcelona' – and he clearly hit the sweet spot with the more sober Norwich & Norfolk Savings Bank, which remains a bank to this day. He also designed his own offices, on the corner of London Street, and now part of the Jarrold department store (see ch. 46), where Skipper didn't pass up the opportunity to remind the world of his craft, incorporating a series of friezes on the outside of the building showing him and his staff hard at work, and even his wife visiting one of her husband's buildings.

Address Earlham Cemetery, Earlham Road, Norwich NR2 1BH | Getting there Buses 21, 22, 23 and 24 stop near Earlham Cemetery | Hours Daily 8am–dusk | Tip If you're a fan of Skipper, the next place to visit is the seaside resort of Cromer, a short train ride away on the North Norfolk Coast, where his Hotel De Paris magnificently dominates the seafront; Skipper is also responsible for several other structures around the town.

39 __ The Great Hospital

A remarkable collection of buildings from various eras

Founded in 1249 by Bishop Walter de Suffield to provide care for elderly priests and the poor, the Great Hospital is a remarkable complex of buildings from various eras. It's focused on an original 13th-century core, which after almost 800 years remains the home of over 100 elderly Norwich residents of limited means. There's a good chance you won't have seen anything like it before, and the good news is that you can gain access on regular monthly tours.

Tours take in the grounds of what is basically the fanciest and most fascinating sheltered housing estate you'll ever see, and it's not just the original buildings that make it special. The house of Thomas Ivory is a Georgian gem built by the Norwich architect as his own home in 1752. Elsewhere there's a historic 'swan pit' built by Ivory's son William, and Edward Boardman's medieval-style Birkbeck Hall, which mimics the 15th-century beamed refectory across the hall. Study the carved dragons in the wooden spandrels here before exiting onto the delightful cloisters, said to be one of the smallest in the country, dated 1450.

From the cloister, access the original building of the Great Hospital – basically a church – divided between the men's ward in the nave, the women's ward in the chancel and the original church of St Helen between the two. The church is full of fascinating detail, most prominent of which are the coloured bosses on the vaulting of the south transept, showing monarchs, saints and other scenes. The two-tiered women's ward has been left pretty much as it was when the last residents left in 1980, with period furnishings and other knick-knacks decorating the living and sleeping cubicles, that are pretty much as they were in the 16th century. Known as the Eagle Ward, its ceiling is decorated with over 250 eagle emblems of Anne of Bohemia, first wife of Richard II, who visited Norwich in 1383.

Address Bishopgate, Norwich NR1 4EL, www.greathospital.org.uk | Getting there Bus to Tombland; 10-minute walk from the railway station following Riverside Road, crossing Bishop Bridge and following Bishopgate | Hours Tours run on the first Wednesday of every month between April and October. They start at 10am and last around 90 minutes. | Tip If you enjoyed viewing the bosses on the church vaulting, be sure not to miss the bosses in the nave of the cathedral and in particular the cathedral cloisters, some of which are remarkable – showing pagan figures, weird creatures, feasting and thievery, visions of hell and even two defecating medieval men.

40__Gressenhall Farm and Workhouse

Victorian workhouse open to the public

Around 20 miles east of Norwich, Gressenhall Farm and Workhouse is one of only three Victorian workhouses in the UK currently open to the public. In some ways it's a museum of Victorian rural life in Norfolk, and worth visiting just for that, with displays of farm implements and machinery and all manner of objects relating to Norfolk's countryside: tools, toys and crockery, patched-up farm labourers' clothing and old photographs of rural locations. But its best displays focus on the time it served as a workhouse, from a late 18th-century 'House of Industry' for the poor, its conversion to a workhouse after the 1834 Poor Law, and its eventual closure in 1948. All of which are accompanied by affecting personal stories that whisper gently from the whitewashed walls.

You can see the laundry, with its original steam-powered machines and drying racks, the men's exercise courtyard, complete with the inmates' graffiti, and the dungeon, where inmates were sent if they broke the rules. Outside you can visit the brick-and-flint chapel and a schoolroom, which all the workhouse children would have had to attend, mock-ups of village businesses, such as post office, general store and blacksmith's, along with kitchen and wildlife gardens. There's also an orchard on the workhouse's old burial ground, and an adventure playground beyond.

Stroll across the road to visit Gressenhall Farm. Purchased by the original House of Correction in the 18th century, it's a working farm run on traditional lines by volunteers, with Suffolk Punch horses, rare breed pigs and a barn full of old farm implements. You'll also have the chance to jump on Gressenhall's own tractor-pulled trailer. The farmhouse itself is worth a peek, kitted out as in Victorian times, while afterwards you can take a lovely walk across the fields and back along the river.

Address Gressenhall, Norfolk NR20 4DR, +44 (0)1362 869 263, www.museums.norfolk.gov.uk | Getting there Bus to Dereham, then transfer to bus 21 to Gressenhall; by car, a 25-minute drive from Norwich | Hours Mar–Oct, daily 10am–5pm | Tip A new footpath runs from the workhouse three miles to nearby Dereham, a delightful and easy hour-long walk that connects the Wensum Way and Nar Valley Way.

41 The Guildhall

Serving many significant roles for centuries

A handsome flint and stone building from the early 15th century, the Guildhall was the first thing built after the city was granted its charter. Deliberately reminiscent of the sort of town halls and official buildings found on market squares of Dutch and Flemish towns, it's a fascinating and diverse place, has served a variety of purposes over the years – tollhouse, prison, police station, court room, town hall and public records office – and when it was built was the largest and grandest civic building in the country.

In the basement you can visit the cells – in use until the 1980s – a weird mix of medieval arches, brickwork and modern additions. Through a fabulous studded original oak door, the Gothic vaulted and whitewashed undercroft, the oldest part of the 15th-century building, is where Robert Kett is said to have been kept before his trial in 1549 – as was the 16th-century heretic Robert Bilney, before being burned at the stake at Lollards Pit.

Upstairs are three court rooms-cum-council chambers. One, on the ground floor, the galleried Court of Record, was until recently a café and is now used as offices for the Norwich & Norfolk Festival. Above this, the 'Sword Room' was the original medieval court space and is now decorated in Victorian style. Displaying the judge's throne on high, the defendant's pen and public gallery, and lots of wood panelling, it was used as a court room until the 1970s. Tours also include the impressive Council Chamber, with benches, stained glass recycled from a chapel below (now the Norwich sheriff's office, and off limits) and a 15th-century ceiling that includes the earliest depiction of the Norwich lion and castle emblem. It feels a very historic space, and perhaps the most surprising thing is that it was still in use less than a century ago – it was only superseded by the much larger council chamber in City Hall in 1938 (see ch. 23).

Address Guildhall Hill, Norwich NR2 1JS | Getting there Lots of buses stop nearby; 10–15-minute walk from the railway station | Hours Roughly two free guided tours a month – hours vary – plus open on Heritage Open Days and other special occasions | Tip The Guildhall is currently home to the offices of the Norwich and Norfolk Festival, one of whose main venues, Norwich Arts Centre, occupies another converted building a 5-minute walk from here, the church of St Swithins, which was voted Britain's best small venue a few years ago.

42 Gybsons Conduit
Grand public water fountain

Gybsons Conduit is a funny little thing, tucked away down an alley on the west side of Westwick Street, facing the riverside development of Anchor Quay. The first structure to be restored by the Norwich Preservation Trust, it's an elaborate and rather grand public water fountain – an outlet of an ancient well – built in 1578, funded by wealthy local brewer and sheriff of Norwich Robert Gybson. At the time, Gybson was keen to construct something to benefit the local community so he could gain permission to build on the land adjacent to the fountain, which originally stood on the other side of Westwick Street, next to the church of St Lawrence (it was also known as 'St Lawrence's Well').

Gybson was not only a shrewd operator, he was a vain one too, making sure that his generosity was not forgotten by generations to come, not only by making his water source a perfect little example of Renaissance architectural style, with a curvy pediment, coats of arms and suchlike, but also by adding a little rhyme that among other things reminds everyone that his 'coste…' was '…not smal'. It also mentions that having built the fountain he should fear 'No Foes' – suggesting that in building the fountain he had effectively made sure that the city's most influential people were on his side. Ironically, he later became extremely unpopular with the city authorities and was stripped of all his civic decorations. He died in 1606, and is buried in the church of St Lawrence.

The fountain has been moved at least twice – once, in the 1860s, when it was set into a wall of Bullards Brewery, and more recently, when the Anchor Quay houses were built on the site of the brewery in the 1980s (there's a Bullard's sign on the wall). To get to it, walk through the entrance in the brick wall on the north side of Westwick Street and take the steps down.

Address Anchor Quay, Westwick Street, Norwich NR3 3XP | Getting there Five-minute walk from Market Place; 15–20-minute walk from the railway station | Hours Always visible | Tip From Gybsons Conduit you can cut through and cross the Wensum by St Miles or Coslany Bridge. There has been a bridge here since the 12th century, although the current iron version dates from 1804. It's one of Norwich's most picturesque spots but was in fact at the heart of the city's industrial area. The building with the arch on the right, just before the bridge, was part of Bullards brewery, as you can see from the sign on its side – viewable from the other side of the river.

43___Gyre & Gimble
Original gin at the city's best cocktail bar

There are more brands of craft gin than you can shake a stick at these days, but Gyre & Gimble is from Norwich. What's more, there's a lot more than gin-making to Gyre & Gimble's innovative owners, Craig Alison and Rory Sutton. First of all, they run a terrific cocktail bar on Charing Cross, where they also make their gin – before your very eyes in fact, in what is perhaps the city centre's most practically useful window display. Push the door and climb the stairs and you'll find the cocktail bar on the right – a surprisingly light, bright space with a retro, speakeasy vibe. Sit down and you'll be served at your table with one of G&G's excellent cocktails – each of which is named after their main ingredient and made in their own particular style: 'Olive' is basically an extremely dirty Martini, 'Tomato' a spicy Bloody Mary, but refined with a perfectly clear tomato consommé. Perhaps most popular are the 'Negroni Flights' – basically a series of mini Negronis of your choice.

The guys soon outgrew the cocktail bar and distillery and recently opened another premises in the Royal Arcade (see ch. 78), selling the city's best range of spirits – think rare tequilas and weird Italian artichoke drinks – along with their own gins. There are several varieties of these, for example Coastal Gin, made with botanicals foraged on the North Norfolk Coast, Cherry Gin, and a special 'Pinot Noir' gin, which is made in collaboration with Bungay's Flint vineyard. They also sell craft beers from a variety of local breweries along with a selection of really interesting wines.

Best of all you can attend one of their weekend Gin Academies to make your own gin using the botanicals provided. You get to take a bottle away and they keep the recipe so you can go back and buy more. You also get to drink lots of gin and tonic during the process, so it's always fun, whatever the quality of your concoction!

Address 14 Charing Cross, Norwich NR2 4AL (Cocktail Bar & Distillery), +44 (0)1603 625119; Shop 6, Royal Arcade, Norwich NR2 1NQ (Gin Academy & Shop), +44(0)1603 622797, www.gyreandgimble.co.uk | Getting there Five-minute walk from Market Place; 15–20-minute walk from the railway station | Hours Cocktail Bar daily 4pm–1am; shop daily 10am–7pm | Tip Norwich is home to other craft ginsmiths, among them the distinctive ceramic bottles of Norfolk Gin, made by husband-and-wife team Jonathan and Alison Redding, and Bullards Gin, revived in 2015 by the great-great-grandson of the original Norwich brewer.

44 The Halls

St Andrew's and Blackfriars – important city venues

Flanking the open space north of St Andrew's Street, 'The Halls' together make up one of Norwich's most impressive medieval buildings – basically the country's most complete surviving medieval friary complex, and also one of the city's largest and most important venues.

The Halls are St Andrew's Hall and Blackfriars Hall, each of which was part of a mid 15th-century church for the Dominican friars, built to replace an earlier structure that was unfortunately destroyed by fire. You can see from the outside on St Andrew's Plain that it was basically one enormous building. Funded by the Paston family and Thomas Erpingham, whose son was a friar here, the friary survived demolition by Henry VIII a century later by agreeing to adopt a dual purpose as a public venue – a deal brokered by the mayor of the time, Augustine Steward. It was later used as the city council's official chapel, and was the church of the Dutch-speaking refugees from the Low Countries from the latter part of the 16th century. During the 18th and 19th centuries, it was used as the city's workhouse.

St Andrew's Hall formed the nave of the original church, where the public would worship, while Blackfriars was the choir, where only the friars were allowed; off to the sides are the former cloisters, the crypt and the slightly sad remains of Beckett's Chapel – one of the few relics from the previous 13th-century building – covered by a plastic roof. The halls themselves are relatively bare, and you're well aware of the day-to-day business of the place, with a bar separating the two, and a stage set up in St Andrew's Hall. Visit for the sense of space in each hall, St Andrew's fine hammerbeam roof, and the portraits of Norwich mayors through the centuries, the oldest of which are in Blackfriars Hall, including two misattributed 16th-century portraits of Augustine Steward and Robert Carver.

Address St Andrew's Plain, Norwich NR3 1AU, www.thehallsnorwich.com/blackfriars | Getting there A short walk from Market Place; 10–15-minute walk from the railway station | Hours Mon, Wed & Fri 11am–3pm, other times for events – check website for current information on visiting | Tip The minister for the church's Dutch-speaking congregation in the early 17th century was one Johannes Elison, whose portrait (along with that of his wife, Mary) was painted by Rembrandt in 1634 and hangs in Boston's Museum of Fine Arts – the only known Rembrandt portrait of someone resident in England.

45 Horning
Picturesque riverside village

Just a few miles downriver from Wroxham, the village of Horning sits on a sharp bend in the Bure. It is in many ways the quintessential Broadland village, with a couple of pubs and a terrific fish restaurant, a picturesque village green overlooking the staithe and a busy, boaty vibe through most of the year.

Horning features prominently in a couple of Arthur Ransome's tales of kids' derring-do on the Broads – *Coot Club* and *Big Six* – both of which evoke the Broads' mysterious emptiness at a time when it was becoming busier than ever with boating traffic. The view over the almost right-angle turn of Horning Reach from the tables of the Swan pub remains one of the Broads' most iconic scenes. There are worse ways of spending a few hours than sitting here, gazing at the seemingly never-ending marshes opposite, and watching the river traffic pass gently by.

Once you've wandered around here for little while, you've pretty much seen most of what Horning has to offer, but the village's long main street extends down the river for another mile or so, past a series of pretty dykes and thatched boathouses and cottages to Ferry Marina. Here you can find more moorings and another pub: The Ferry Inn – a venerable old place that has been long mooted for a never-quite-realised upgrade. You can rent a boat here, or take the foot ferry across to the far bank, where a boarded path leads to Cockshoot Broad. Alternatively, follow the road up towards Ranworth and Salhouse.

From the centre of the village you can also take a path across the fields to the complex of former RAF Neatishead, which hosts the RAF Air Defence Radar Museum – a labyrinth of rooms and corridors that was a key centre of operations during both World War II and the Cold War years. If you prefer something a little more active, the popular theme park of BeWILDerwood can be found in the other direction (see ch. 10).

Address Lower Street, Horning, Norfolk NR12 8AA | **Getting there** Regular buses from Castle Meadow; train to Wroxham & Hoveton, then a 5-minute taxi ride; by car, a 25-minute drive from central Norwich | **Hours** 24 hours | **Tip** Horning also offers short excursions deeper into the Broads on its Southern Comfort riverboat tours; these leave from the Swan, and are an easy and painless way to explore the river, with tea and scones and an engaging commentary.

46 Jarrold Department Store

'As Norwich as Colman's Mustard or The Canaries'

You can't get more Norwich than Jarrold, the city's beloved department store, which started down in Suffolk in 1770, and 50 years later moved to Norwich. Jarrold used to be a major local publisher, bookseller and printer – as evidenced by its own print works by the river and the fact that it successfully published best-selling titles such as Anna Sewell's *Black Beauty* in 1877 (see ch. 4), and later became a major publisher of calendars and visitor guides. These days the focus is mainly on its retail offering, which occupies an ornate ('baroque' according to Pevsner) premises on the corner of the Market Place, which was renovated and extended by the most sought-after local architect of the day, George Skipper, in 1903.

Locals love Jarrold. It's a properly independent company, still family owned and run, and as well as being a terrific store, it's involved in all sorts of community endeavours. Like most department stores, it sells just about everything, but it does so with style, celebrating its heritage while at the same time never being afraid to move with the times – something that is clear in the classy nature of its fashion, furniture, book and other departments, and its superb basement food hall, which was massively upgraded in 2022. In a nod to its past, it has a lovely and very useful art, print and stationery store in a nearby building on the corner of Bedford Street, and is also home to a number of cafés and restaurants, varying from a terrific wine bar in the food hall to a seafood restaurant on floor two.

Jarrold feels like a store that has been serving the city for the best part of two centuries, and its offices occupy one of the most historic buildings in the city in the nearby St James Mill on the river (see ch. 74), yet it's for the most part as fresh and contemporary as if it opened for the first time only yesterday. As Stephen Fry said, Jarrold is 'as Norwich as Colman's Mustard or The Canaries'.

Address 1-11 London Street, Norwich NR2 1JF, +44 (0)1603 660661, www.jarrold.co.uk |
Getting there Bus to Castle Meadow; 10–15-minute walk from the railway station | Hours
Opening times vary throughout the year but generally are Mon–Wed & Fri 9.30am–5pm,
Thu 9.30am–5.30pm, Sat 9.30am–6pm, Sun 10.30am–4.30pm | Tip George Skipper
occupied offices on the upper floor of the redbrick extension on London Street, which he duly
decorated with decorative carvings illustrating himself and his builders at work. Anna Sewell
also gets a name check along with other writers on the upper façade.

47 __ Jem Mace
Norwich's famous bare-knuckle fighter

Two minutes' walk from the market in the centre of Norwich, tiny Swan Lane is home to a gaggle of jewellers, but is perhaps more notable for a plaque that remembers one James – or Jem – Mace: Mace's pub, the Swan Inn, gave the street its name, and he was an internationally-renowned boxer during the 19th century.

Mace started out as a violin player, and it was only when he was attacked while busking in Great Yarmouth that he discovered his fighting skills. Boxing was a tough sport in those days: fights were bare-knuckle and usually fought outside; they could also go on indefinitely, sometimes as long as 50 rounds, or as long as both men could stand.

Jem Mace was not only a successful fighter, he also did a lot to refine and professionalise the sport, pioneering techniques that are still followed today. For example, he used a skipping rope to improve balance, and emphasised the importance of footwork rather than standing still – a technique that was widely seen as cowardly at the time. For a while he toured as a fighter with Pablo Fanqué's circus (see ch. 67), taking on all comers – and playing the violin between bouts!

Mace became heavyweight champion of England after a £50 fight on Canvey Island, but when bare-knuckle fighting was banned in this country, he travelled to America. He became heavyweight champion of the world after a hard-fought victory in 1870, when he won $2,500, a vast amount of money then. He was by this time internationally renowned in the world of boxing. He trained young boxers, ran a bar in New York, and even carried on fighting well into his 70s, before returning to Norwich to run the Swan Inn. He was also a gambler, however, and had frittered away his money long before his death in 1910. Yet Mace remains a big name in the world of boxing, revered by the likes of Mike Tyson, and inducted into the boxing hall of fame in the 1950s.

48_Jenny Lind

The cause of 19th-century 'Lind-Mania'

Stockholm soprano Jenny Lind – 'The Swedish Nightingale' – was discovered at the age of 10 when a maid overheard her singing to her cat. The maid told her mistress, principal dancer at the Royal Opera House, and soon afterwards Lind was offered a scholarship to the Royal Swedish Opera School. By her early 20s she was dazzling audiences across Europe. The cream of society flocked to see Lind's London debut in 1847; an enraptured Queen Victoria even threw a bouquet from the royal box. 'Lind Mania' ensued, her face and name appearing on everything from snuff boxes to soap.

Lind's association with Norwich began with a visit in 1847 as part of a national tour. She received a rapturous welcome, accompanied by the ringing of church bells. She returned in 1849, staying with Edward Stanley, Bishop of Norwich, and his wife Catherine, close friends who encouraged Lind's philanthropic bent. This time, two sell-out concerts in St Andrew's Hall were fund-raisers for the city's poor, and led to the opening of the Jenny Lind Infirmary for Sick Children in 1854 on the south side of Pottergate. The handsome red-brick house at 76 (a private home known as Jenny Lind House) is all that remains of the original buildings, but a plaque commemorates the hospital.

In 1900 the new Jenny Lind Hospital for Children opened on Unthank Road, on land donated by Norwich mustard scion Jeremiah Colman. One of the buildings still stands, but the hospital has since moved to the Norwich & Norfolk Hospital. The foundation stone from Unthank Road remains on the site, but the modern hospital is perhaps the most fitting memorial to a woman who used her talent to help children. As Lind herself said: 'Of all the money God allowed me to give away when my poor throat could call an audience to listen to its production, none has borne a nobler or more genuine fruit than The Jenny Lind Hospital in Norwich.'

Original site
of the infirmary for sick children
established in 1853 by the Swedish soprano
Jenny Lind
1820-1887
In 1900 the infirmary was transferred
to Unthank Road

Address 76 Pottergate, Norwich NR2 1DZ | **Getting there** Bus to Castle Meadow; 10-minute walk from the railway station | **Hours** Always visible, but please be mindful of residents' privacy | **Tip** Just east of Unthank Road on Vauxhall Street, a marble arch that reads 'Jenny Lind Play Ground for Children' was moved here from Pottergate where it marked the entrance to a playground on the site of the old hospital.

49 Kett's Heights

Best view of the city from a historic location

Without doubt the biggest uprising in Norfolk during Norwich's glory years as England's second city, Kett's Rebellion of 1549 originated in Wymondham. It was triggered when a small band of peasant farmers protested about land enclosures, which restricted access to common land. Informally led by a yeoman farmer called Robert Kett, and his brother William, the protest gathered momentum on their march to Norwich, picking up thousands of followers, who famously gathered on Mousehold Heath in July 1549 to besiege the city.

Robert Kett was the rebels' charismatic leader, and he set up camp here for almost two months with some 13,000 men. It's fair to assume that their encampment covered quite a wide area, but Kett's Heights is fondly remembered as its epicentre. Formally known as 'Kett's Castle', it's also proof (if any were needed) that Norfolk is not entirely flat. Looking better than it has done for some time thanks to the efforts of the Friends of Kett's Heights, you can see the remains of some terrace gardens, next to which are the remains of St Michael's Chapel, built by Bishop Herbert de Losinga as a replacement after he bulldozed the church of St Michael in Tombland. But what really steals the show up here is the panorama of central Norwich, which is by far the best in the city, and the cathedral so close you feel as if you could almost touch it. It was from this place that Kett drew up his famous '29 Requests', which were fruitlessly presented to the Earl of Somerset in July 1549.

In between bouts of bargaining, Kett led his men into the city on two occasions – once at the end of July, when they won a pitched battle with the forces of the Marquess of Northampton on what is now Palace Plain, and on 29 August, when they were forced to retreat by forces led by the Earl of Warwick; Kett was captured, imprisoned and eventually executed.

Address Kett's Hill, Norwich NR1 4EZ | **Getting there** It's a short climb to Kett's Heights from the roundabout at the end of Bishop Bridge Road, following Kett's Hill for around 100m, then the path to the right | **Hours** Always accessible | **Tip** There's another reminder of Kett's Rebellion on the road between Wymondham and Hethersett, 'Kett's Oak', where Robert Kett is said to have addressed the rebels before marching on Norwich.

50 Lollards Pit

Once a place of execution, now ale and good cheer

The Lollards were a 15th-century sect of the established Church, followers of one John Wycliffe, a 14th-century cleric who believed the traditional hierarchical form of the Church required reform. Their name comes from the Dutch for gravedigger, but they were basically believed to be heretics, pure and simple: they rejected the theory of transubstantiation (whereby bread is transformed into the body of Christ and wine into His blood), not to mention the practices of baptism and confession. As such, they were regarded with suspicion pretty much everywhere they went.

Lollards were most numerous in East Anglia, when in the first half of the 15th century around 50 men and women were tried and convicted of heresy and either flogged or executed at Lollards Pit. Later, in 1531, the controversial Lutheran preacher Thomas Bilney was burned there after languishing in the Guildhall dungeons, while many more were executed during the reign of Henry VIII's daughter Mary – 'Bloody Mary' as she came to be known – when deviations of any kind from established Church dogma were not tolerated in a bid to re-establish papal supremacy in England.

These days there's nothing to see of Lollards Pit, but it's not difficult to imagine this as a perfect place for such gruesome events, being located outside the boundaries of the city at the time, and easy to reach from the castle or guildhall dungeons by way of Bishopgate and Bishop Bridge. A plaque on the riverbank remembers Bilney and name checks several others who met their deaths here during Mary's reign – worth a look before retiring to the only other memorial, the Lollards Pit pub on Riverside Road, where the Lollards are commemorated with a plaque on the wall. And the pub? It's a 15th-century structure that's now a thoroughly convivial watering-hole serving a particularly good range of local ales!

Address **69-71 Riverside Road, Norwich NR1 1SR** | Getting there **Five-minute walk from the railway station** | Hours **Plaque always visible** | Tip **Just across Bishop Bridge on the city side of the river, The Red Lion is a similarly convivial pub and a lovely waterside place for a drink or bite to eat.**

51 Loose's Emporium

Packed full of items you didn't know you needed

Talk to anyone who has lived in Norwich for a while about shopping, and the one place they will always mention is Loose's. Suitably located on raffish Magdalen Street, it's probably the longest-running and most revered retail establishment in the city – and with good reason. If any one shop deserves to be referred to as an 'Aladdin's Cave', it's Loose's – a truly vast and fascinating hotch-potch of antiques, bric-a-brac, vintage and collectible items of all kinds that gives real meaning to the suggestion that one person's junk is another person's treasure.

Spread across two fabulously cluttered floors, and made up of over 60 different stalls and enterprises, Loose's is Norwich's largest location for discovering antiques and collectibles, and has no doubt been the venue for many an afternoon lost to retail reveries. This remarkable emporium is crammed full with everything from genuine antique furniture to leftover house-clearance items, crowds of blonde-haired, smiling Barbie dolls, vintage bikes and scooters, militaria, vintage clothes and one of the city's most extensive selections of second-hand books, located on the first floor in 'Undercover Books'. Anything second-hand rules the roost! Our canine companions are also welcome in Loose's Emporium – provided they're kept on a lead – and there's even a small café where you can sit down, have a cup of tea and admire your haul after a hard day's rummaging.

Loose's is the ultimate antidote to all those fancy gift shops that stock lots of things no one needs, offering an inexhaustible supply of unique items you didn't know you needed, but that you can't help but crave once you're here. It's ideal for sourcing that unusual gift. Guard that wallet or purse closely when entering this den of temptation: even the most miserly of visitors finds it incredibly difficult to leave without buying something!

Address 23–25 Magdalen Street, Norwich NR3 1LP, +44 (0)1603 665600 | Getting there Several buses go down Magdalen Street; 15–20-minute walk from the railway station | Hours Mon–Fri 10am–5pm, Sat 9am–5pm, Sun 11am–4pm | Tip The spirit of Loose's continues across the road in the King's Head, a lovely old pub with a good variety of real ales, a bar-billiards table and not a gastropub item in sight.

52 Lotus Cars

Essential visit for any F1 fanatic

Sports car marque Lotus Cars has been associated with Norwich and Norfolk for years, and now sponsors Norwich City FC. The company originally took over part of an old RAF base at Hethel in 1966, building a factory and adapting the disused runway as a test track. Lotus was a very successful sports car brand at the time. Its founder, Colin Chapman, was adept at product placement: Emma Peel of cult TV series The Avengers drove a Lotus Elan, and a decade later Roger Moore's James Bond had a submersible Elise in The Spy Who Loved Me. Chapman also built Lotus into a top Formula 1 team, employing drivers such as Jim Clark, Jochen Rindt, Emmerson Fittipaldi and Mario Andretti, who won Lotus' last F1 championship in 1978.

Chapman died in 1982, and the company went into decline, withdrawing from Formula 1 and experiencing falling sales and mounting debts. Ownership passed from Chapman to General Motors, and most recently to Chinese company Geely, which also owns Volvo, Polestar and part of Aston Martin. This has led to a revival of sorts, with the iconic light roadster, the Elise, proving particularly popular. The plant was also used by Elon Musk as the base for the Tesla Roadster, and the sleek, new Emira – to be the company's last petrol-driven car – and several other top-secret electric vehicles, are set to launch over the next few years. Automation and more efficient working practices have increased annual production from around 1,500 to 5,000 cars, but Lotus remains an essentially low-volume, high-quality car maker, retaining Chapman's focus on top-quality engineering, aerodynamics and handling.

Join one of the factory tours, the best of which – the so-called Heritage tours – include the museum of Team Lotus, where the Formula 1 cars are on display. Thrill-seekers can also join one of Lotus' regular track days, which include various tours, and the chance to take a car on the track.

Address Potash Lane, Hethel, Norwich, Norfolk NR14 8EZ, www.lotuscars.com/en-GB/ factory-tours | Getting there By car, a 20-minute drive from the centre of Norwich – there's no public transport | Hours Factory Tours Mon–Thu 9.30am & 1.30pm; Heritage Tours Tue & Wed 9.30am & 1.30pm | Tip For something completely different, go for a circular walk in the woods – soothing for the soul after the rigours of the production line, and with a real possibility of seeing a deer or two springing through the trees.

53 Macarons & More

Masterchef finalist finds niche in Norwich

Opened a decade ago by Masterchef finalist Tim Kinnaird, Macarons & More fits Norwich's elegant Royal Arcade (see ch. 78) like a glove. It's a small shop, but you can't help notice the colourful displays of French macarons in its always immaculate windows. This in turn makes it almost impossible to resist at least sticking your nose around the door – indeed a visit here could be the perfect present to yourself after a hard day's shopping in Norwich city centre.

Tim Kinnaird used to be a doctor, working as a consultant paediatrician at Norwich & Norfolk hospital. But he made his name during the Masterchef series of 2010, when he wowed the critics and presenters with his superb sweets and desserts. As John Torode said at the time: 'Tim has the gift of making sweet things incredibly delicious – and his macarons are to die for.' Not surprisingly, after the programme had finished it was a no-brainer for Tim to give up his doctoring role and move into the food industry, and soon afterwards he started his own business, baking his beloved French-style macarons and selling them online. This swiftly grew, and before long Tim opened his own shop, along with a separate bakery. From here they also run a popular cookery school, offering classes that aim to create new legions of budding Bake Off contenders, and there's a second retail outlet, in the Chantry shopping centre. They've won numerous awards over the years, including 'Indy Retailer of the Year' in the Observer food magazine.

There's a huge range of macarons to choose from, including cappuccino, pistachio, praline, salted caramel and many more. They're sold individually, as well as in boxes of six or twelve. Giant macarons, macaron towers, brownies, celebration cakes and other delectable items are also available – all as beautifully packaged and served as you would expect from one of the city's best local indy businesses!

Address 11 Royal Arcade, Norwich NR2 1NQ, www.macaronsandmore.com | Getting there Bus to Castle Meadow; 10-minute walk from the railway station | Hours Mon–Fri 10am–5pm, Sat 9.30am–4.30pm, Sun 11am-4pm | Tip Those with a sweet tooth might want to drop by one of Norwich's more traditional bakeries, Ketts Hill Bakery, right by Kett's Heights, where they have been baking cakes, buns, bread and savouries for around 200 years.

54 Maddermarket Theatre

Home of the Norwich Players

Tucked away on St John's Alley between Pottergate and St Andrew's Street, the Maddermarket Theatre has seen lots of different uses. Built as a Catholic chapel dedicated to St John the Baptist in the late 18th century, and later used as a factory, grocery, and a meeting place for the Salvation Army, it was rescued from dereliction by the Guild of Norwich Players in 1921, after founder Walter Nugent Monck discovered its excellent acoustics. Monck wasn't from Norwich but, like many before him and since, he visited the city and discovered he rather liked it. He moved to Norwich just before the Great War, living and working here until he died in 1958, and is buried in the church of St John Maddermarket next door (see ch. 92), where there's a memorial plaque. Monck's theatre troupe originally performed at his house at nearby Ninham's Court, and later at one of the most ancient buildings in the city, the Music House on King Street. Neither were especially suitable, and Monck was delighted to find the chapel not only sounded great but also had a ready-made gallery on three sides.

The Maddermarket Theatre opened in 1921 with a performance of *As You Like It* and has remained the home of the Norwich Players ever since, extended in the 1950s to accommodate 300 seats by taking over adjoining buildings. Its foundation and survival are a triumph of independent thinking. As George Bernard Shaw had it, there is 'nothing in British theatrical history more extraordinary than the creation of the Maddermarket Theatre.' It has the distinction of being the first theatre in the world to perform all of Shakespeare's plays under the same producer, although the repertoire nowadays is more eclectic, with a dozen or so productions each year featuring everything from stand-up comedy to musicals. It also has a theatre school and a bar that opens before performances.

Address St John's Alley, Norwich NR2 1DR, +44 (0)1603 620917, www.maddermarket.co.uk | Getting there Bus to Castle Meadow; 10–15-minute walk from the railway station | Hours Open for performances most nights of the week; the bar is open 45 minutes before a performance and remains open afterwards. | Tip Look out for the plaque outside the theatre to the Elizabethan comic actor William Kemp, which commemorates his famous Morris Dance from London to Norwich, in particular his completion of the dance by jumping over the church wall.

55 Magdalen Street

Full of serendipitous opportunity

No visitor to Norwich can spend time in the city without visiting Magdalen Street! It might not look like much, but it has a raffish charm that's simply lacking from the majority of other city centre locations. Above all, it's a place for thriftiness, home to any number of antique and bric-a-brac shops – of which the legendary Looses is only the largest and best-known (see ch. 51). There are also several charity shops, including a supermarket-sized Oxfam outlet, a handful of second-hand record stores, such as Out of Time Records, plus continental food stores and more.

Anchored at one end by Fye Bridge and at the other by the Artichoke pub, it's not an especially pretty street, especially in the stretch straddled by the inner ring road, and the soon-to-be-demolished 1960s disaster/development Anglia Square. But there's something to see at every turn, and it's undeniably full of history. Peek into the passageway at 33 Magdalen Street to Gurney House, the birthplace of not one but two prominent 19th-century feminists – Harriet Martineau and Elizabeth Fry (plaques mark the spot – see ch. 30). Further up the street, the medieval church of St Saviour sports a plaque remembering Matthew Parker, who rose to become Norwich's only archbishop of Canterbury in 1559, and who was a prime influencer during the Reformation. He is, however, best remembered as the original 'Nosy Parker' because of an unfortunate and well-known tendency to pry into other people's business.

The street even has a branch of North Norfolk's iconic department store – Roys (see ch. 80) – and at the very top, a branch of the city's best bakery, Bread Source. You can even stay on Magdalen Street if you wish, at the one-bedroom Gothic House B&B, which just happens to sit right behind the street's best pub, the excellent and unchanged King's Head, which has won 'Norwich Pub of the Year' several times in recent years.

Address Magdalen Street, Norwich NR3 1NF | Getting there Several buses go down Magdalen Street; 15–20-minute walk from the railway station | Hours Always open | Tip Why not try a Magdalen Street pub crawl? Start at The Ribs of Beef, crossing the river for a quick one at The Mischief, then taking in The Kings Head and The Artichoke at the top of the street. If you can, squeeze in a detour down Cowgate to the excellent Plasterers Arms, which has craft ales, great pizza and a unique 'Fem-Ale' festival, dedicated to the womenfolk of the brewing industry! Always drink responsibly!

56 The Maids Head Hotel
'Fantastically rambling but comfortable'

Anchoring one end of Tombland, just across from the cathedral grounds, the Maids Head is Norwich's oldest hotel. Indeed, it claims to be the oldest in the country, dating back to the 1100s, when it served as the palace of the Bishop of Norwich. Visitors are in excellent company. The Black Prince is said to have dined here after jousting in 1359, while about a century later local bigwig John Paston is said to have suggested the name change to the Maids Head. Cardinal Wolsey and Catherine of Aragon lodged here for a while, and the hotel was a popular spot for intrigue and conspiracy during the mid-16th-century Kett's Rebellion – a period evocatively written up in C. J. Sansom's novelisation of the period, *Tombland* (see ch. 85).

Nowadays the oldest parts of the hotel date back to the 15th century, and naturally some areas are haunted, with guests reporting sightings of the so-called 'Grey Maid', a 60-year-old woman in a grey uniform who occasionally appears in the bar, leaving the scent of lavender behind her. There's also a famously unpleasant former mayor of Norwich who is said to be found muttering irritably to himself from time to time.

Rather refreshingly, the hotel is still independently owned, and remains one of the city's most comfortable places to stay, with around 80 rooms, an excellent restaurant and a cosy oak-panelled bar that was in the 1940s a favourite drinking haunt of locally based US airmen. It's a funny old building, with a warren of corridors on different levels conjoining the original coaching inn and an unsympathetic 1960s extension that sticks out into the car park behind. Rooms are all shapes and sizes, varying from nicely furnished, contemporary and spacious doubles to more characterful beamed affairs. As J. B. Priestley said, when he stayed here on his 'English Journey', 'it's a fantastically rambling but comfortable old place.'

Address 20 Tombland, Norwich NR3 1LB, +44 (0)1603 209955, www.maidsheadhotel.co.uk | **Getting there** Purple Line buses to Tombland; 10–15-minute walk from the railway station | **Hours** Always open | **Tip** The hotel famously featured in both the book and the film of L. P. Hartley's mid-20th-century novel *The Go Between*, and also in the P. D. James novel *Devices & Desires*.

57 Marston Marshes
A haven for wildlife all year round

Situated down on the southern fringes of the city, there's not much to dislike about Marston Marshes and the nearby stretch of woodland known as Danby Wood. It's easy to reach – perhaps half an hour's walk from the city centre – and there's a handy car park right by the main entrance. Surprisingly, it's just one of no fewer than eight nature reserves within the confines of Norwich, comprising almost 27 hectares of reed beds, dykes and wet woodland stretching down to the river Yare – a lovely sight at any time of year, and a haven for all sorts of wildlife.

There are a couple of main routes through the nature reserve, and it's quite easy to explore while staying on a well-made path, much of which is suitable for wheelchairs and buggies. The main path leads down to and follows the river Yare for a while, which is relatively narrow at this point, before either turning back into the marsh via a stretch of boardwalk, or following the river further on a less well-made path. On your way you might see a heron or maybe a kestrel, cetti's and other warblers, egrets and snipes, as well as more common birds such as geese, moorhens and redwings. During the summer, dragonflies swoop over the water and grey-green grass snakes lie coiled in the reeds. You might also catch sight of a muntjac deer and even an otter or two if you're careful and quiet. Between May and November, you will also see the cattle that graze on the marshy meadows during these months.

Make some time if you can to wander through Danby Wood, a small atmospheric stretch of undulating woodland that has flourished over the last century or so on the site of an old chalk quarry. A path leads through oak, ash, lime, walnut and sycamore trees, and if you're here in spring you'll find a sprinkling of bluebells in one corner, as well as multiple wildflowers in a natural clearing.

Address Marston Lane, Norwich NR4 | Getting there Purple Line buses go right by Marston Marshes and Danby Woods | Hours Always open | Tip If you want to continue your walk you should follow Marston Lane and then Church Lane for about 500m, towards Cringleford, where at the thatched church of St Andrew you can pick up the Yare Valley Way, which follows the river all the way to UEA and Earlham Park beyond. From there you can either continue to Bowthorpe Marshes across the main road or take the bus back along Earlham Road to the city centre.

58 Mousehold Heath

Classic views from the city's largest open space

Believe it or not, Norwich is a lot like Rome in its layers of history, the way the past is always present in the jumble of architecture and features from multiple eras that make up the city centre. It's also similar in the way you can climb a hill on the edge of the central urban area (within the original walls) and get a terrific view of the city's jagged skyline – which is what you can do from the heights of Mousehold Heath, a relatively wild mix of wood and heathland that sprouts above the north-eastern quarters of the city centre.

The Heath originally reached out into the Broads National Park as far as Salhouse, but this was much reduced in the 19th century when it became a protected area, by which time much of the open heath had become overgrown and wooded. Extending to around 184 acres, it remains an atmospheric spot for a stroll without having to leave the city, and has featured heavily in Norwich's history over the years. Most notably, Robert Kett's famous rebels made their camp on Mousehold Heath in 1549 before attacking the city six weeks later, and it was the inspiration for a number of Norwich School painters, not least John Crome, whose large painting of Mousehold hangs in London's Tate Britain gallery.

Some of the best views over the city are from Kett's Heights (see ch. 49), where there are also the ruins of a Norman chapel, and from Britannia Road, right in front of the impressive remnants of Britannia Barracks, former home of the Royal Norfolk regiment and now part of the city's prison. Further up, Gurney Road takes you deeper into the heath and you can take a variety of trails to explore its wooded valleys from various car parks. A highlight is the spring gathering of mating frogs around Vinegar Pond – actually an old quarry – as well as other features, such as a bandstand and a pitch-and-putt course, as well as a few old ruins and a derelict ranger's house.

Address Heartsease Lane, Norwich NR7 9NT | Getting there Pink Line buses 10, 11 and 12 drop you near the fringes of Mousehold Heath | Hours Always open | Tip There is parking on Gilman Road and also along Gurney Road, where Zak's Diner has been providing refreshment to hungry Mousehold hikers since 1979 (they also have another branch just down the hill, across the river from the Cow Tower).

59 The Murderers

Great pub with grisly history

Situated towards the bottom of Timberhill, a narrow pedestrian street sloping down to Red Lion Street and the heart of the city centre, The Murderers is actually the more familiar nickname for the Gardeners Arms, one of the city's nicest but also more notorious pubs, famous for a grisly murder that took place there in 1895.

Step inside, and you're surrounded by murder memorabilia, with various Easter Daily Press articles telling the story of one Mildred Miles, who was murdered here by her husband Frank Miles in June 1895, when he bashed in her head with an iron peg in a fit of jealous rage. Mildred had gone to live with her mother, Maria Wilby, who was the landlady of the Gardeners Arms, after having been threatened and abused by her husband over a long period. She died of her injuries after several days in hospital – a series of events which is gruesomely described on the walls of the pub.

It was apparently an open-and-shut case – Miles is reported to have said to his wife in the pub, 'God strike me blind, I'll be the death of you in the morning', having aimed a ceramic match stand at her after seeing her with another man the day before. He confessed his guilt to a nearby shopkeeper and was tried and sentenced to be hanged, but following a public outcry his sentence was reduced to life in prison, which in his case meant a mere 10 years. His death certificate of 1905 is displayed on the wall, alongside that of his wife, who clearly didn't get much justice for her murder.

These days, The Murderers is one of the city centre's nicest spots for a pint or a bite, with excellent real ales and good quality pub grub. It's a cosy, beamed old pub with lots of nooks and crannies and live sports on TV. The landlord, Philip Cutter, knows the power of a good story, and pieced together the story of the murder himself, assembling the various exhibits on the walls.

Address 2–8 Timberhill, Norwich NR1 3LB | Getting there A short walk from Castle Meadow; 10-minute walk from the railway station | Hours Daily 11am–11pm | Tip They serve food in the pub, but if you're hungry it might be worth walking around the corner to Benoli, on Orford St, a favourite of food critic Grace Dent, who said 'If this place were closer to my house, I would eat here a lot'.

60 Norfolk Tank Museum

Collection of working tanks and armoured vehicles

Tucked away in the countryside just outside Long Stratton, 14 miles south of Norwich, the Norfolk Tank Museum is a remarkable private collection of tanks, armoured vehicles and small arms. The result of one man and his son's grandiose hobby, perhaps the weirdest thing about it is that it shares a location with a museum in the next village that's the result of another curious obsession (the Forncett Industrial Steam Museum, see ch. 35). Like FISM, the Tank Museum is unique, and well worth venturing out of the city centre to see.

The museum is a big shed basically, home to a collection of military vehicles, tanks and small arms dating mainly from the Cold War period, although a few are much earlier. It's the life's work of Stephen Machaye and his son Aaron, who started collecting tanks and military vehicles back in the 1980s, taking them to fairs and gatherings all over the UK. It was only after a suggestion from their patron, Richard Dannatt, that others might be interested in their collection, that they decided to open the museum, which they did in 2009, with the help of over 50 volunteers.

They have around thirty vehicles in all, all in working order, the 'oldest' being a World War I replica they built for the British motorcyclist Guy Martin for a Channel 4 TV show a couple of years ago. The museum's authentic vehicles, however, date mainly from the postwar era and include a Saladin armoured scout car, a Chieftain battle tank from the 1960s, and a trio of Centurion tanks, one of which was in the first Gulf War. It's a hands-on sort of place, with a selection of Stephen, Aaron and the volunteers on hand to show you around and answer questions, and visitors encouraged to get into vehicles and handle the small arms – a great way for kids to learn how things work and very much in line with the ethos of the museum, which is deliberately more educational than warlike.

Address Station Road, Forncett St Peter, Norwich NR16 1HZ, +44 (0)1508 532650, www.norfolktankmuseum.co.uk | Getting there By car, around half an hour's drive from central Norwich – no public transport available | Hours Easter to end-Oct Tue–Thu, Sat 10am–5pm | Tip Enthusiasts might like to know that Norfolk has a second tank museum, up in Weybourne on the North Norfolk coast.

61 Norwich Castle

Many ghastly happenings – and an art gallery

Still undergoing a massive restoration, Norwich Castle is an impos-
ing presence, towering above the centre of the city. The first English
castle to be built on an artificial mound, it was constructed around
the same time as the cathedral during the latter part of the 11th century. However, it was never really used as a royal palace, nor was the
magnificent steadfastness of its keep tested, and it became a prison
in the 13th century – which it remained for around 500 years.

As a prison, Norwich Castle saw many ghastly happenings, most
notably the hanging of the rebel Robert Kett in 1549 (see ch. 49).
But despite the restoration of the keep from its Victorian hybrid,
these days it's mainly visited as a museum, home to a series of galleries entered from a central, rotunda-like extension. These hold
displays of Roman finds from Norfolk, in particular from Caistor
St Edmund and Gayton Thorpe, as well as lots relating to Boudicca
and the Iceni tribes from what is now Norfolk. The museum also
has galleries displaying Anglo-Saxon finds, decorative arts and natural history, including lots of Victorian-style stuffed beasts and
some beautiful dioramas of various Norfolk landscapes, complete
with sound effects.

The museum's real pride, however, is its Colman art collection,
which focuses on the 19th-century Norwich School of painters – a
group of artists who spent their time painting landscapes and scenes
of everyday life in their native East Anglia. The collection of Jeremiah
Colman, supplemented by that of his son, Russell James Colman, in
1946, is a vision of Norfolk recognisable today, with lots of naturalistic landscapes by the movement's two leading lights, John Sell Cotman
and John Crome, along with rustic scenes of Great Yarmouth by Joseph
Stannard and some late-19th-century depictions of old Norwich by
David Hodgson and Henry Ninham.

Address Castle Street, Norwich NR1 3JU, +44 (0)1603 493625, www.museums.norfolk.gov.uk | Getting there Lots of bus routes terminate at Castle Meadow; 10-minute walk from the railway station | Hours Mon–Sat 10am–4.30pm, Sun 1–4.30pm | Tip Don't miss the amazing 'double portrait' of Amelia Opie by her husband John Opie of 1798, in the decorative arts gallery.

62 Norwich Cathedral

The city's most iconic structure

Norwich is a city of medieval churches – it once had 58, of which 31 remain – but there is no building more symbolic of the city than the cathedral, its spire rising over 300 feet. Originally a Norman structure, it was built in 1096 under the city's first bishop, Herbert de Losinga. Entry is by way of a modern extension, which links the cathedral proper with the cloister and the refectory café. Inside, marvel at the thickness of the Norman pillars of the nave, which soar towards the later Gothic fan vaulting of the ceiling, on which the bosses tell the story of the Old and New Testaments. While viewing these is difficult, two mirrors positioned in the nave help a little.

Outside the choir, a tomb displays a skeleton bearing the words 'As you are now even so was I. And as I am so shall you be'. Further on are several chapels, not least that of St Luke, home to the five-panelled Despenser Reredos – a painting showing the Flagellation, Passion, Crucifixion, Resurrection and Ascension of Christ, which only escaped the Reformation's destruction by being used as a worktable. Also visit the Bauchon Chapel, for its memorial to the MP and abolitionist Thomas Buxton, and the bishop's throne – dating back to the eighth century, beneath which is a recess filled with relics.

There are more remnants of the ancient cathedral in the nearby reliquary arch, in the form of traces of the building's original medieval wall paintings, which help to decorate the cathedral treasury. On the other, north side of the building, a door opens on to the glories of the cathedral's cloisters, the only two-storey cloisters in England. Built between 1297 and 1450, they are decorated with another set of intricately sculpted bosses, showing scenes from the Apocalypse among many other, more worldly scenes. Best of all, though, is the relative peacefulness of the cloister and its views of the spire rising high above.

Address 65 The Close, Norwich NR1 4DH, www.cathedral.org.uk | Getting there Purple Line buses to Tombland; 10–15-minute walk through the cathedral precincts from the railway station | Hours Daily 7am–6.30pm | Tip Join one of the free tours of the cathedral which run on the hour, every hour (Mon–Sat 10am–3pm).

63 __ Norwich Market

Street food heaven at UK's largest, oldest market

Norwich is so often about superlatives, and nowhere more so than at its market, which has been in its current location since shortly after the Norman Conquest, making it the UK's longest-running permanent market by some way. It's also the largest daily market in the UK, and may be Norwich's most beloved institution, eclipsed only by the city's football team.

Flanked on one side by City Hall and The Forum, and on the other by Gentleman's Walk and the Royal Arcade (see ch. 78), with St Peter Mancroft dominating on the southern edge and the alleys of The Lanes disappearing beyond the Guildhall, the market feels like the city's true centre. Most of its 200 or so stalls are open every day except Sunday. The market thrives almost in spite of the city council, which not so long ago replaced its old-fashioned stalls with permanent metal shuttered structures. These weren't particularly popular, and give a slightly too-uniform appearance to what is basically a collection of jobbing traders. There is talk of loosening things up a bit, and the entrepreneurial spirit of the marketeers, combined with the enduring affection and support of Norwich folk, seems to be winning out, with the market on a bit of a roll in recent years, not least due to its burgeoning collection of street food options. Quite simply, the market is a terrific place to eat, with everything from great fish and chips to Chilean empanadas and churros to hog roasts and American barbecue on offer for the hungry visitor.

What else can you buy? Well, just about anything, really! Luggage, ex-military clothing, second-hand books and household essentials, as well as retail food items like great bread and pastries (Bread Source), loose-leaf teas (Birchley's), cheese (The Cheeseman) and craft beers (Sir Toby's), plus of course The Canaries are represented on the market by the enduring 'On the Stall City' stall.

Address Market Place, Norwich NR2 1ND, www.norwichmarket.net | **Getting there** Bus to Castle Meadow; 10–15-minute walk from the railway station | **Hours** Mon, Wed & Fri 8am–5pm, Tue, Thu & Sat 10am–7pm | **Tip** A lot of the market's stalls provide stools or chairs and tables, making a perfect lunch-stop; plus, there are plenty of benches at the top in front of City Hall or obliging pubs such as The Garnet, which make a point of welcoming market grazers – as long as they buy a drink!

64 Norwich Puppet Theatre

Disused church put to good use

Few cities have as many medieval churches as Norwich, but the city has a knack of finding a function for those that are no longer in use – and there's perhaps no better example of this than Norwich Puppet Theatre! Founded in 1980, this occupies the church of St James the Less, a landmark building with an odd polygonal tower, not far from the cathedral, on the city's inner ring road. You can't miss it as you drive into Norwich from the direction of Wroxham.

The theatre stages productions developed by its own company, as well as by visiting puppeteers and touring companies, in a 165-seat auditorium fashioned out of the church's old nave. The theatre produces shows for both adults and children – everything from puppet pantomimes at Christmas to innovative takes on classic stories such as Thumbelina and The Enormous Turnip. Attending a production at Norwich Puppet Theatre is a rather magical experience, whether or not you're bringing children... Visitors enter into the art of theatre in what is a truly atmospheric environment.

The Puppet Theatre also works with local schools and runs puppeteering workshops and regular classes, and stages other events based around the craft of puppetry, theatre and drama. Famously, one of the theatre's principal puppeteers, Ronnie Le Drew, starred as Tom Hanks' double in a recent Disney remake of Pinocchio. More recently, the theatre hit the national news when (with the help of an Arts Council grant) they restored their old puppeting steel 'bridge', which sits high above the stage out of sight of the audience. This has made it possible to once again stage performances with old-fashioned wire and string-controlled marionettes, rather than glove or stick puppets, and has expanded the company's repertoire enormously. Is there a better use than this for one of Norwich's many disused medieval churches? We can't think of one!

Address St James the Less, Whitefriars, Norwich NR3 1TN, www.puppettheatre.co.uk |
Getting there Lots of buses stop close by | Hours Shows and workshops every week; check
website for current details | Tip If you're thirsty before or after a puppet theatre performance,
it's worth knowing that one of the city centre's best pubs, The Leopard, is a short walk away
on Bull Close Road. They serve lots of good local and international ales – on draft and in
bottles – host pop-up food vendors and even provide plates and cutlery if you want to bring a
takeaway. Be warned, though, that it's a kid-free space later on in the evening.

65 Octagon Chapel

Georgian home of Norwich's Unitarians

One of the most impressive buildings on historic Colegate, just to the north of the Wensum, is the Octagon Chapel, designed for the Unitarians by Thomas Ivory in the 1750s to a demanding brief by the minister at the time, Dr John Taylor, who raised over £5,000 from the congregation to pay for it. It's clearly a special building from the moment you walk in, built for worship in the round, and with a circle of windows making a typically light and bright Georgian structure. It all centres on the pulpit, which is surrounded by a balcony and organ, both of which were added later; the ground floor is filled with box pews, while there's a balcony to accommodate additional worshippers. These days a congregation of around 60 meets here every week, and unsurprisingly the building is also used for regular concerts, recitals and other events – indeed it would be a shame if it were not.

The Unitarians lie somewhere between the Quakers and the Congregationalists (whose own flagship place of worship, The Old Meeting House, is also on Colegate, a few doors down, see ch. 66). They sing recognisable hymns, albeit with their own words, and see themselves as seekers of spirituality outside the confines of organised religion. There are no prayers or regular rituals, and they consider the Bible just one of a number of sacred texts. Perhaps the biggest clue to the openness of the Unitarian mind is the roundel below the organ, which displays symbols of many of the world's major religions – among them a cross, a crescent, a Star of David, even a wheel for Buddhism, all centred on a chalice or candle. If proof were needed that Unitarians tend to be free thinkers, consider their most famous advocate in the 19th century, Harriet Martineau – an abolitionist known for her writings on society, race and feminism, whose brother James was hugely influential in the Unitarian movement.

Address 23 Colegate, Norwich NR3 1BN, +44 (0)1603 666636, www.octagonchapel.co.uk |
Getting there The best way to get to the Octagon Chapel is to cross the river on Blackfriars Bridge,
follow St Georges Street from there and turn right on to Colegate. | Hours Fri 11am–1pm |
Tip The creator of the UK's first non-denominational cemetery, Thomas Drummond, also
worshipped here, and it was in the chapel's churchyard his wife was buried, before being dug up
and moved to be the first occupant of his new Rosary Cemetery, close to Norwich station.

66 — The Old Meeting House
The best hidden church in Norwich

Since the arrival of 'The Strangers' in the late 16th century, Norwich has been a city of non-conformists and free thinkers – famously home to an assortment of Quakers, Congregationalists and Unitarians, whose places of worships are still scattered around the city centre. Of these, the Old Meeting House is one of its most notable, known as the 'best hidden church in Norwich', as it's almost entirely out of sight at the end of a short lane off Colegate. Like its close neighbour, the more accessible Octagon Chapel, it's a perfect example of the open, non-conformist, Congregationalist churches that became popular after the end of the 17th century.

The church was founded by a dissenter who had previously fled to The Netherlands – William Bridge – a former rector of St Peter Hungate and St George Tombland (see ch. 82). Norwich was at the time bursting with free-thinking folk, who, after the Act of Toleration of 1689, were at liberty to build their own places of worship. Constructed in 1693, the redbrick, Georgian-style Meeting House – as it was known then – is the impressive result, and the only pity is that it's so hard for non-worshippers to visit.

The church became known as the Old Meeting House after the construction of the Octagon Chapel 50 years later, just down the street. You can look at the exterior and the small garden at the back at any time, admiring its large, well-proportioned windows and Corinthian pilasters, but access to the interior is a different matter. If you are lucky enough to gain entry, you'll find that it's a classic of its kind, roughly square in shape and beautifully proportioned, with box pews on the ground floor and seating in a gallery upstairs orientated towards the high pulpit in the centre, accessed by a staircase on either side. It feels like a real oasis of peace and calm, simplicity and civilisation, within the modern city.

Address Colegate, Norwich NR3 1BW, +44 (0)1603 436658, www.oldmeetinghousechurch.org.uk | Getting there The best way to get here is to cross the river on Blackfriars Bridge, follow St Georges Street from there and turn right on to Colegate – the Old Meeting House is just past the Octagon Chapel and Martineau Hall. | Hours Services every Sun at 3pm | Tip The city's other Old Meeting House is the Quaker place of worship just off the Market Place on Upper Goat Lane, where Elizabeth Fry would have attended services. Still in use today, it is hard to gain access but their meetings for worship take place on Sundays at 10.45am, and sometimes on Wednesday lunchtimes.

67 Pablo Fanque Plaque

Circus man of extraordinary equestrian skills

A few doors down All Saints Green from the John Lewis department store in the centre of Norwich, Pablo Fanque House is an odd name for a block housing a mixture of student flats and offices. But its namesake was a true celebrity in this part of town during the mid-19th century – a mixed-race man who, as an unusually skilled equestrian, became the first black circus owner in Britain.

Pablo Fanque remains a relatively mysterious character. No one knows for sure when or where he was born, but the consensus is that he was born in Norwich in 1810, into a large family, the son of an African man who came to the city to work as a servant. His real name was William Darby, and he worked in the circus from the age of 11. Developing skill as a horse rider and tightrope walker, he gradually made his name as a performer of note, being written up in the Illustrated London News as having 'extraordinary horse-training skills', not to mention an extraordinary horse! Later, he started his own circus, touring Britain and Ireland to enormous acclaim, inducting his children into the company and starting to hold benefit performances for other performers – the Beatles derived 'Being for the Benefit of Mr Kite' from a playlist for a performance in Rochdale in 1843 for 'Pablo Fanque's Circus Royal, when said Mr Kite was billed to appear 'on the tightrope' alongside Mr Henderson, who was to perform 'trampoline leaps and somersaults'!

Fanque spent a lot of time touring the north of England, before his death in Yorkshire in 1871, and is now buried, alongside his wife, in Leeds. There's a blue memorial plaque opposite All Saints church on the side of the John Lewis building, close to where he used to live – though of course the most popular memorial may prove to be the Beatles song itself, whose deliberately carnival atmosphere paints a nostalgic and enthralling picture of Fanque's vanished world.

Address All Saint's Green, Norwich NR1 3LX | Getting there 5-minute walk from Castle Meadow; 15-minute walk from the railway station | Hours Always accessible | Tip Pablo Fanque is further remembered across the street from John Lewis, where the modern block of Pablo Fanque House provides sumptuous accommodation for Norwich students.

CASTLE

Pablo Fanque
1810-1871

Pablo Fanque, real name William Darby, the first black British circus proprietor, was born in Norwich and lived near to this site. He is immortalised in the Beatles song Being for the Benefit of Mr Kite, with the line:

'The Hendersons will all be there, late of Pablo Fanque's fair, what a scene!'

NORWICH
HEART

68__Palace Plain

Home of Norwich's best-known landscape painter

A triangular space between the river Wensum and the cathedral, Palace Plain – named after the Bishop's Palace, the entrance to which is on its far side – represents a good jumping-off point for all sorts of mighty Norwich attractions – Tombland (see ch. 102), the Bishop's Garden (see ch. 11), and the famous Adam & Eve pub (see ch. 1) and Great Hospital. It was also home to one of the greatest British landscapists of the 19th century after Constable: John Sell Cotman.

Cotman lived in a Georgian house on the north side of the square. As the plaque attests, Cotman was one of the pioneers of the Norwich School of painters, and a tremendously prolific painter in his own right. He particularly specialised in watercolours, travelling the country painting landscapes in Wales and Yorkshire, and hobnobbing with artistic contemporaries like J. M. W. Turner. Cotman eventually washed up in Great Yarmouth, where he worked as a teacher, and made drawings and etchings of Norfolk churches and villages. He moved to this rather grand house in 1823, where he lived on and off for 20 years – struggling to survive, battling depression and financial difficulties until his death in 1842. Truly the life of an artist in many ways!

Palace Plain is only one of several 'Plains' in the city centre. Norwich is unique in using 'Plain' – an Anglicised version of the Dutch word 'Plein' – meaning 'Square' or 'Place', and this is just one of the city's many legacies of the influx of Flemish and Dutch immigrants during the 16th and 17th centuries. Cotman's painting – and that of John Crome and the Norwich School in general – was another, adapting the realistic landscape styles of Dutch painters such as Ruisdael and Hobbema to the Norfolk locales they were most familiar with. See the best collection of their work anywhere, in the Colman collection at Norwich Castle museum (see ch. 61).

JOHN SELL COTMAN
1782 – 1842
One of the most famous
of the Norwich School
of Painters

Lived in this House

Address Norwich NR3 1RW | **Getting there** A short walk from Tombland or a 15-minute walk from the railway station – the nicest route being along Riverside Road and up Bishopgate. | **Hours** Always open | **Tip** A few doors down from the Cotman house, the Wig & Pen provides a pleasant spot for a drink or bite to eat, while on the opposite corner, St Martin at Palace is a very old church (originally of Saxon origins) but one with a mixed history, closing in 1971 and later becoming HQ of the probation service in Norwich. It's now the home of the Norwich Historic Churches Trust, and open a couple of days a week.

69 Philip Browne

Norwich's streetwear and designer clothing pioneer

Norwich has far more cool designer menswear stores than you would expect in a city of its size. This is partly down to Philip Browne, who set a marker when he opened his own city centre store in 1986. A former engineer with a taste for sharp clothes and offbeat style, Philip has from the beginning basically sold stuff he liked: unable to attract the biggest fashion names back in the 1980s, he instead focused on new and up-and-coming designers such as Alexander McQueen and John Galliano, mixing their creations with street and sportswear brands. Back then, Philip was a pioneer, and made a name for himself with a pick-and-mix approach to fashion, often blending formal wear with casual clothing items. Among many other things, he once even suggested it might be a good idea to try wearing a tailored suit without a tie – a concept so shocking at the time that it was featured as a local news item!

Browne is one of a band of cool, creative Norwich folk hailing from Great Yarmouth, and his maverick status lives on to this day; it's not just a shop, Browne maintains, but a 'place of refuge for music, art and discussion'. This is not only manifest in the up-to-the-minute, often hyper-pricey brands stocked – as well as established brands such as Dries van Noten, Comme des Garcons and Moncler, the shop has always championed young British designers – but in the shop itself, which displays 20th century British art by the likes of Peter Blake, Damien Hirst, and local artist Colin Self. It's also known for off-the-wall window installations, which do much more than just display clothes – indeed, sometimes they don't even bother with that! Meanwhile, upstairs, Philip's mate Wink runs a thriving tattoo parlour, while above that a posse of Browne acolytes beaver away, staging fashion shoots, packing up orders and running the Philip Browne website and publishing operation.

Address 3 Guildhall Hill, Norwich NR2 1JH, +44 (0)1603 664886, www.philipbrowne.co.uk | Getting there Bus to Castle Meadow, from where it's a short walk across the Market Place | Hours Mon–Sat 9.30am–5.30pm | Tip If you're lucky, the shop might have a copy of its '1001 Pieces of Shit' on display: a sumptuous celebration not only of Browne and his shop, but of design in general!

70___Plantation Garden

Landscaped gardens offering peace and seclusion

Almost next door to the city's Catholic Cathedral, the Plantation Garden is an out-of-the-centre attraction worth crossing the ring road for. Quite simply, this is one of Norwich's best-loved sights: a set of landscaped gardens that were conjured out of an old chalk quarry from the middle of the 19th century onwards, and which now provide one of Norwich's most peaceful and secluded spots.

The land for the gardens used to be occupied by the city's Victorian gaol (see ch. 15 and ch. 20), and was originally left by one John Pettus to provide an income to pay for priests at the cathedral and church of St Simon & St Jude, where there is a monument to him and his father. The chalk quarry was later leased by the local retailer and cabinet maker Henry Trevor, who was successful enough to build the Palladian-style Plantation House itself next door, after which he leased the quarry land to serve as his gardens.

The gardens follow the contours of the quarry, with neat and synchronised beds at the bottom and walkways and paths climbing up the side and occasionally across the gardens, which are planted with a mixture of traditionally English and sub-tropical plants and shrubs. It's a fairy-tale kind of place: there's a Gothic-style fountain, promenades and enticing vistas. Stone arches, balustrades and fragments of ancient buildings only add to what feels like a gloriously rustic escape a million miles from the nearby inner ring road.

It's hard to believe, but after Trevor's death in 1897 his garden was largely forgotten, became rather neglected, and was eventually abandoned. It was only rediscovered and revamped in the 1980s, when the Plantation Garden Preservation Trust was set up. It still has something of the feel of a secret garden, but in fact is anything but: accessible for just a small fee, it's probably Norwich's most life-enhancing little corner.

Address 4 Earlham Road, Norwich NR2 3DB | Getting there Bus 26 passes right by the garden | Hours Daily 9am–6pm | Tip Just around the corner from Plantation Garden, the Georgian Townhouse is a revamp of a rough old place that now makes a good place for a drink or a bite to eat, with a wide-ranging menu that takes in burgers and fish and chips, steaks and vegan dishes, afternoon tea and Sunday roasts.

71 Pottergate

A study in miniature of what makes Norwich special

One of Norwich's most ancient thoroughfares, Pottergate is also one of its most appealing, the main spine of the city centre district known as The Lanes – a set of narrow streets and alleys that is a perfect place to browse interesting stores, buy a gift or window-shop designer outfits, and grab a good cup of coffee or bite to eat. A stroll along Pottergate is essential on any visit to Norwich, a study in miniature of what makes the city so special.

First is Seven Wolves, brother store to Dogfish on nearby Bedford Street, and as good an example of any of how unusually well supplied Norwich is with high-end men's casual clothing stores. Just beyond is the church St John Maddermarket (see ch. 92), and the Maddermarket Theatre behind (see ch. 54). Beyond here are two long-established shops that are typical of this part of town – Norfolk Yarn and Head in the Clouds; the former is a family-run enterprise specialising in wool, yarn and crafts, and running regular knitting and crochet workshops, the latter a delightful hippy-dippy establishment that claims to be Britain's oldest headshop, selling fashion, jewellery, oils and incense, magic and, er, 'cannabis culture' items. Across the street, Yard offers excellent pasta dishes, while further down you'll see another clothes shop devoted to blokes' fashion – Mod One, stacked full of Fred Perry shirts, button-down collar shirts, fine knitwear, tailored trousers and other 60s retro styles.

A few yards along, the Grosvenor Fish Bar is a Norwich institution, cooking up great fish and chips for the best part of a century, as is Strangers Coffee opposite, which serves terrific coffee, and roasts and sells its own artisan beans. The building on the next corner is a fine art deco pub that's been through many incarnations (including Lauren Gregory's late and lamented Birdcage – see ch. 37) and is now the slick Drawing Rooms bar.

Address Pottergate, Norwich NR2 | Getting there Bus to Castle Meadow, then a five-minute walk | Hours Accessible 24 hours | Tip Just off Pottergate on Exchange Street, the unique self-service Wallow Wine Bar is a tempting place to rest and recuperate after a shopping spree. Or try L'Hexagone, a tiny, thoroughly French restaurant on Lower Goat Lane.

72 Pub & Paddle

A unique way to see the city – and its pubs

Time was that you could drink in a different Norwich pub every night of the year and not visit the same place twice. King Street alone is said to have once been home to 50 pubs, and breweries too were everywhere, from Bullards Anchor Brewery on Westwick Street to the Crown Brewery on King Street. Nowadays, Norwich is an altogether more sober place, but it's still a city of great pubs, and you have to visit at least a few while you're here.

A unique way to do this is available from the folks at Pub & Paddle: they rent out lovely wooden Canadian canoes from a pontoon next door to the Ribs of Beef – itself one of the city's most scenically situated pubs, perched by the river on Fye Bridge, and with a very nice riverside terrace overlooking the water that makes a pleasant place to while away a summer's afternoon. You can still enjoy the views of the river from any of its three rooms and they do a good range of ales and also serve some of the city's best burgers, among other things.

Having hired your canoe, you can paddle upriver towards Blackfriars Bridge and the excellent bar of the Norwich Playhouse, and beyond there as far as the old Bullards brewery at New Mills Yard. Alternatively, go in the opposite direction, down towards Bishop Bridge, where the Red Lion makes a pleasant stopover. You can also head out of the city centre altogether, past Whitlingham (and the junction of the Wensum and the Yare rivers), stopping off at the riverside pubs of Thorpe St Andrew, like the Rushcutters Arms, before turning back – making a 4- to 5-hour round-trip in total. If you want to, you can paddle even further out into the Broads, stopping at pubs such as the Ferry House at Surlingham and Coldham Hall, opposite Brundall. This is a one-way trip, but the good news is that the kind folks at Pub & Paddle will pick up your canoe, while you get a taxi back into the city.

Address 24 Wensum Street, Norwich NR3 1HY, www.pubandpaddle.com | Getting there
A short walk from Tombland | Hours Apr–Oct, daily 10am–8pm | Tip If you like the idea
of getting out on the river, you could also try Norfolk Paddleboards, on the river next door
to the Red Lion pub (https://www.norfolkpaddleboards.com), or The Canoe Man, opposite
the railway station (www.thecanoeman.com).

73 __ Pull's Ferry

John Pull: ferryman and innkeeper

One of the most picturesque sights along the river Wensum in central Norwich is an old flint and stone structure known as Pull's Ferry, located a short distance from the Bishop Bridge on the city centre side. Formerly a water gate built to serve Norwich Cathedral, a canal (long since filled) ran from here during Norman times to deliver the materials used to build the Norman cathedral – stone from Caen in France, as well as timber and iron from the Baltic region and Scandinavia. The tower and the slipway are all that survive from that period today, however.

For several centuries both the canal and the gate continued to be used to ferry goods up to the cathedral precincts (see ch. 21), and during the 15th century an arch was built across the canal to help provide security, creating the basic structure that can be seen today. A century or so later, the Ferry House was added on the western side, given impetus by the dissolution of the cathedral's monastic community. From the end of the 18th century the building became a destination point for ferries that ran across the river, and home to the ferryman who operated them – one of whom, John Pull, was the ferryman for almost 50 years during the 18th century, and also ran the building as an inn. It's amazing but true, considering there are two bridges within a hundred metres of this location, that ferries continued to run across the river here into the 1940s!

Pull's Ferry is as pretty as a picture, and inevitably features in just about every Norwich tourist brochure you'll see. Although best viewed from the other side of the river, it's a nice place to linger on a riverside walk from the station into the centre of the city (see ch. 74), and also a starting point for the stroll up Canal Road past the playing fields of Norwich School to the very heart of Norwich, the cathedral and its unique precincts.

Address 29 Ferry Lane, Norwich NR1 4DZ | Getting there Five-minute walk from the railway station, following the riverside path from the Compleat Angler pub | Hours Accessible 24 hours | Tip Pull's Ferry is a good place to start on a walk along the Wensum, following the path past the Red Lion pub to the Cow Tower, and all the way up to Blackfriars Bridge, by the Norwich Playhouse (see ch. 74).

74 Riverside Walk

Historic meander from station to city centre

Norwich is full of great walks, but there's nothing quite like a stroll along the Wensum, which girdles the south-western part of the city centre, and provides an intriguing and picturesque stroll from the station, with lots of historical interest along the way.

To start, cross the road and bridge from the station and take the steps down by the Compleat Angler pub. The footpath leads from here to Pull's Ferry and Bishop Bridge just beyond – a pedestrian-only bridge dating from around 1340 – and was once a key route into the city. Stop for refreshment at the excellent Red Lion pub, or carry on to where the river bends north at the Cow Tower. This isn't part of the original city walls, which didn't extend to this part of town, but was built in 1399 to house artillery and defend approaches to the city from across the river, as you can see from the slender gun ports high up on the walls.

The path continues from here towards the next bridge at Palace Plain, where Kett's rebels repelled the king's forces in 1549. On the north side of the river, you can't miss St James Mill, built in 1839 on the site of a former Carmelite Friary and the last hurrah of the city's venerable textile trade. It's now the headquarters of Jarrolds (see ch. 46), whose printing presses used to be housed in the mill's various outbuildings (now subject to a major redevelopment).

Continue to the next bridge, past colourful riverside houses to the Ribs of Beef pub at Fye Bridge, where 'scolds, strumpets and witches' were once punished on the city's ducking stool. This is a good pit-stop before continuing to Blackfriars Bridge, designed and built by Sir John Soane in 1784. On the left, see some ruinous remnants of the vast Blackfriars complex among the buildings of the former Norwich Technical Institute (now University of the Arts); on the right across the bridge, the bar of Norwich Playhouse makes a good place to stop!

Address Norwich NR1 1NS | **Getting there** The start of the walk is right opposite the railway station, through the terrace of the Compleat Angler pub | **Hours** Daily dawn–dusk | **Tip** You used to be able to visit the machinery and artefacts of the Jarrold Print Museum in St James Mill, but this has since been moved to a permanent exhibition at the National Trust's Blickling Hall, 14 miles north of Norwich.

75 ROARR!
Dinosaur Adventure
Fun-filled dino-destination for kids of all ages

Just over 10 miles north-west of Norwich, ROARR! Dinosaur Adventure is one of the city's most popular children's attractions, and – so they claim – the largest dinosaur-themed adventure park in the UK. It's easy to reach by car, open all year round, and offers a range of things to do for kids of all ages. It is a potentially fun-filled day out for anyone with even a passing interest in dinosaurs!

The core of the park is the Valley of the Dinosaurs, basically a very pleasant woodland walk that takes in lots of models – some animatronic, all with sound effects of some kind – of various species of dinosaur, including all the household names (velociraptors, a giant brachiosaurus, triceratops, a T-Rex) as well as some that would be familiar to only the most serious dinophile. The path winds down through the trees, your stroll accompanied by the roars and cries of the dinos along with the odd neigh or moo from the nearby fields. There are also Rope Walks (zip wires and rope walkways) and a small section devoted to more mundane present-day animal life – everything from cuddly guinea pigs and rabbits to wallabies, pigs and goats.

From here you can take a different route back up through the woods on the Neanderthal Walk, which takes you past creatures from a much later prehistoric era – sabre-toothed cats, woolly mammoths and ultimately a family of the first humans living happily in a cave. Nearby, the park's theatre shows regular film shows and other events, and also houses a soft play area and café. Elsewhere, there are all sorts of things for kids to clamber about on, a dino-themed mini-golf course, and during the summer the Splash Zone mini water park, which offers water slides, swings and all sorts of watery fun. Finally, don't miss the dinosaur-sized gift shop on the way out – it's absolutely ROARRsome!

Address Lenwade, Norfolk NR9 5JE, www.roarr.co.uk | Getting there By car, a 30-minute drive from central Norwich | Hours See website for details | Tip Lenwade is close to the junction of the Marriott's Way, a 26-mile footpath that follows the route of two disused railway lines between Aylsham and Norwich, and the Wensum Way, which runs 12 miles to Gressenhall Workhouse (see ch.40).

76 Roger Hickman's

A restaurant of choice for a night out in Norwich

For years the fine-dining standard in Norwich was set almost singlehandedly by a restaurant called Adlards, which occupied this site on Upper St Giles Street. Chef-patron David Adlard brought high-end cuisine to Norwich, earning a Michelin Star and training up newbies such as Tom Kerridge and Aiden Byrne along the way. His last head chef, Roger Hickman, took the reins in 2010, and basically continued where Adlard left off, maintaining its status as Norwich's restaurant of choice for a special night out, but with his own take on fine dining – a position it has been forced to share after being challenged by a handful of newer fine-dining options, including Richard Bainbridge's place, Benedicts, just around the corner (see ch. 9).

Norwich may have improved as a food destination in recent years, but Hickman, who previously worked with Tom Aikens in London, has continued what he was doing and is still doing it pretty well. Even though he says he really wanted to be a fireman, he's collected no fewer than three AA rosettes. The restaurant is a simple, relatively small space – basically two inter-connected rooms, nicely lit and with tables well-spaced and laid out with white tablecloths for an intimate dinner. It's not a place to get raucous, but neither is it too formal. A three-course fixed menu is on offer at lunchtime, and a choice of a five- or seven-course tasting menu in the evening.

The taster menus come with wine suggestions for each course, a chef's appetiser to start and the odd treat between courses. The choices change with the seasons – for example, think confit duck with textures of garlic followed by loin of venison with a chunk of venison pie, finishing up with chocolate and blood orange mousse: all intricately prepared and presented, but with the simple natural flavours of top-notch ingredients shining through. Happy days for haute-cuisine in NR2!

Address 76 Upper St Giles Street, Norwich NR2 1AB, +44 (0)1603 633522, www.rogerhickmansrestaurant.com | Getting there Five-minute walk from Market Place | Hours Tue–Sat noon–2.30pm & 7–10pm | Tip Upper St Giles packs quite a few more foodie delights into its short stretch of Georgian houses and shopfronts, with various shops of interest including the excellent St Giles Pantry, which specialises in all sorts of delicious Norfolk products.

77 Rosary Cemetery
UK's first non-denominational cemetery

Tucked away behind Norwich city centre's railway station, Rosary Cemetery is Norwich's Highgate, the first non-denominational cemetery in the UK, set up by one Thomas Drummond and laid out on the site of a former market garden. A Presbyterian minister, who preached in Ipswich and at the Octagon Chapel on Colegate, Drummond was eager to find somewhere to accommodate those of different faiths and those who hadn't been baptised, and purchased the site in 1819 with a legacy of £3,000. The cemetery proved very popular, and the initial five-acre site was filled before the end of the century with no fewer than 18,000 burials. The cemetery was later extended by five acres to the north.

It's an extraordinary place, easy to miss despite occupying a big chunk of land in Norwich's south-east corner. Criss-crossed by paths that weave between the gravestones and memorials that are often wreathed with creepers and surging undergrowth, there's a real pleasure in aimlessly strolling its grassy paths and overgrown avenues, studying the names and dates on the stones.

The first person to be buried here, in 1821, was Drummond's wife, Ann, who died in childbirth; her husband joined her in 1852. There are plots devoted to many of Norwich's famous names – Jeremiah Colman heads up the Colman clan's plot, while there are also markers for the printer and retail baron John Jarrold and the architect Edward Boardman (see ch. 79), who designed the chapel. Other notable plots include those of circus proprietor John Barker, the Norwich obstetrician and eye surgeon Emmanuel Cooper, whose family mausoleum is one of the grandest here, and the grave of Norwich shoe business mogul and Lord Mayor, Henry Holmes, which lies under a scramble of brambles up against the fence near the entrance. Holmes was also responsible for converting the Bridewell prison to the museum it remains today.

Address Rosary Road, Norwich NR1 4DA | **Getting there** Five-minute walk from the railway station | **Hours** Daily 9am–4pm | **Tip** Top off your visit to the cemetery with a visit to the Coach & Horses around the corner on Thorpe Road – brewpub of the local Chalk Hill microbrewery. It's a friendly old place with good pub food and a beer garden, and brews its beer on the premises.

78 Royal Arcade

George Skipper's splendid Art Nouveau landmark

Designed by notable local architect George Skipper and opened with much ceremony in 1899, this magnificent example of Art Nouveau architecture is a popular shopping destination, and couldn't be more central. It replaced the Angel Inn which stood here until it was replaced by Edward Boardman's new Royal Hotel on Agricultural Hall Plain in 1897. The most popular of several coaching inns here at that time, notorious for its spicy entertainment and raucous political meetings, you can still see the bust of an angel above the entrance on Gentleman's Walk.

Carefully restored recently, the Royal Arcade is every inch a turn-of-the-century building. It's 75 metres long, with a fully glazed roof, impressive tile work, coloured brickwork, decorative wrought iron and stained glass. Elegant arches with leaded lamps provide a sheltered cut-through to Castle Street, and there's a short spur off to the side, opening out onto White Lion Street.

It wasn't always like this. A few years ago, the arcade looked tired and tatty, with several empty shopfronts, and was somewhere people sheltered from the rain rather than visiting to shop. But new owners have injected fresh life and purpose, and it's now home to some of Norwich's most interesting and creative outlets and businesses, including the fabulous Gyre & Gimble gin academy (see ch. 43), fancy florist Basil & Pip, Lauren Rose interiors, Tim Kinnaird's Macarons & More (see ch. 53), and the wonderful Yalm food hall, which brings together some of Norfolk's finest food and drink producers under one roof, and is almost a destination in its own right (see ch. 111). Pleasingly, there are also a few old favourites that have been here for years, such as Marmalades coffee shop and Langleys Toys. You feel that George Skipper would be pleased that the Royal Arcade is back to its best, and that 120 years on, it's once again the retail landmark he intended.

Address Norwich NR2 1NQ | Getting there 10–15-minute walk from the railway station, and less than five minutes from its bus station and main city centre bus stops | Hours Sun–Wed 8am–7pm, Thu–Sat 8am–11pm | Tip Much of the Arcade's impressive tile decoration is the work of one W. J. Neatley, who, as Royal Doulton's chief designer, also designed the famous tiled food halls at Harrods in London and much else besides.

79 Royal Hotel

Designed by prestigious architect Edward Boardman

One of Norwich city centre's busiest city intersections, Agricultural Hall Plain, is also home to some of its most monumental buildings – the redbrick HQ of once mighty Anglia TV, the neo-classical Post Office (which was also occupied by Anglia TV for a while) and, perhaps grandest of all, the former Royal Hotel. None of these structures are used for their original functions, and they are in various states of disrepair. The Royal Hotel is perhaps the saddest, however, because it's probably the flagship structure of great 19th-century architect, Edward Boardman.

Boardman is a key figure in the history of Norwich. Having set up his practice in 1860, he later became the city's mayor, and was responsible for the conversion of Norwich Castle (see ch. 61) from a gaol to a museum. He also built the grand complex of the Norwich & Norfolk Hospital in 1882 – now converted to some of the city's poshest flats. Boardman also designed a number of Norwich's Methodist churches, including Boardman House, now home to the University of Arts, the United Methodist Church on Chapelfield Road, and the folksy Rosary Chapel, at the entrance to Norwich's first non-denominational cemetery (see ch. 77). His practice was based in Old Bank of England Court off nearby Queen Street, where you'll see the name of 'Edward Boardman, Architect' elegantly etched into the brickwork.

The Royal was state of the art when built in 1897: a beautiful redbrick structure, six storeys high, and as grand a place to stay in central Norwich as you could find, with sumptuous suites, a fancy first-floor restaurant, billiard room and an entrance hall to compare with the most magnificent hotels of London and Paris. But it was conceived at the end of the grand hotel era, and by the 1970s had become an anachronism. Nowadays, it houses a handful of offices and a variety of bars, none of which do justice to their unique location.

Address 25 Bank Plain, Norwich NR2 4SF | Getting there 10-minute walk from the railway station | Hours Always visible | Tip Boardman's son, Edward, later took over the business, and married local mustard heiress Florence Colman, moving to the arts and crafts style house he had built at How Hill – now a study centre for The Broads, and whose beautiful riverside grounds you can still visit.

80_Roys of Wroxham

'The biggest village store in the world'

In business since 1895, Roys of Wroxham is a Norfolk retailing legend. The con-joined villages of Wroxham and Hoveton, divided by the river Bure, are widely known as the gateway to the Broads National Park, and it's here that Roys has served visitors to this popular boating spot for over a century.

The various buildings of Roys almost make up the entire village centre of Hoveton, and take in a two-storey department store, large supermarket, and various outposts around the village, including a garden centre, DIY store and toy shop. Wroxham/Hoveton is a bustling but not especially attractive place, and Roys hasn't really helped, dominating the main drag with overbearing, utilitarian buildings and car parks. But it does make the village a useful place to visit for just about anything, and means that it is busy at most times of day. Also, little can take away from the village's attractive waterside location, bisected by the river Bure, lined by boat rental establishments, restaurants and pubs with terraces overlooking the water.

Roys was founded in 1985 by brothers Arnold and Alfred, in nearby Coltishall. But it was the Hoveton store, which opened four years later, that prospered most. It benefitted from a position on the railway line to the popular seaside town of Cromer, and the then-burgeoning boat hire businesses, catering to holidaymakers eager to explore the Norfolk Broads. Eagle-eyed when it came to spotting an opportunity, the Roys' business grew and grew, until later, under Alfred Roy's son Fred, the 1960s fashion for out-of-town shopping was embraced, leading to some of the smart new buildings and car parks you see today. Fred died on Christmas Eve 1974 – he is memorialised by a slightly tacky plastic water well stuffed into a corner of the café – and was succeeded by his brother Peter, whose children Edward and Paul run the business today.

Address Stalham Road, Hoveton NR12 8DB, www.roys.co.uk | Getting there Train to Wroxham & Hoveton; regular buses from Castle Meadow stop right outside Roys | Hours Mon, Tue & Sat 9am–6pm, Wed–Fri 9am–8pm, Sun 10.30am–4.30pm | Tip Regular guided boat trips down the Bure leave from Hoveton Riverside Park – tickets are available from the Broads National Park information centre nearby.

81 The Sainsbury Centre

The Jewel in UEA's Crown

Built to house the art collection of Robert and Lisa Sainsbury, the Sainsbury Centre for the Visual Arts – on the western fringe of UEA's campus – is the first public building designed by Norman Foster, who came up with its cube-like design in 1973, when the Sainsburys donated their collection to the university.

Foster went on to become Britain's favourite public architect, and aspects of his design for Stansted Airport's terminal are shared with the Sainsbury Centre, which he nicknamed 'The Shed'. But, as Foster also maintained, it's the client that makes a building, and this place was designed to provide a soothing, neutral space for the Sainsburys to display their fabulous art – and it's free!

The Sainsburys began collecting fine and applied art in the 1930s, and were rich enough to develop varied and adventurous tastes while at the same time knowing what they liked. As a result, the collection is both diverse and harmonious, hosting everything from Tang dynasty sculptures to works by Francis Bacon – a great friend of the Sainsburys. Most of the works are figurative, all sculptures displayed so they can be viewed from every aspect – a stipulation of the Sainsburys. Lighting is carefully controlled, partly by Venetian-style blinds that line the walls and ceilings.

Among several works by Bacon is his portrait of Pope Innocent X (after Velasquez's portrait in Rome), which the couple stopped him slashing in a drunken rage after a night out in Soho (you'll notice the bottom right corner is missing), and a couple of stark, dark portraits of Lisa. There are works by other British modernists – Frank Auerbach, John Davies and Henry Moore – while non-British pieces include works by Van Gogh, Chaim Soutine, Modigliani, Giacometti and Jean Arp. There are sculptural pieces from Aztec Mexico, Africa and Egypt, including a remarkable 17th-century bronze head from Benin.

Address Norfolk Road, Norwich NR4 7TJ, +44 (0)1603 593199, www.sainsburycentre.ac.uk | **Getting there** Blue Line buses 25 and 26 to UEA | **Hours** Tue–Fri 9am–6pm, Sat & Sun 10am–5pm | **Tip** Be sure to step outside – to look back at the building and its extraordinary Crescent Wing extension, added in 1999, and to follow a tour of the gallery's outdoor sculptures, dotted around the gallery and the nearby lake (ask for the walking tour leaflet). There's also a terrific shop, a restaurant that makes the most of the building's floor-to-ceiling glass walls, and the centre also hosts regular, high quality temporary exhibitions.

82 __ Saints George and Peter Hungate

Churches featuring beautiful stained glass

At the bottom of Princes Street, just off Tombland, St George is a pretty, mainly 15th-century church, set in a small garden. Occasionally open to visitors, it's still used for worship on Sundays, and it's definitely worth peeking inside if you can to see the stained glass, some of which is contemporary with the church, and a couple of 17th-century tombs. One of these, the tomb of the unforgettably named Alderman Thomas Anguish, captures him kneeling alongside his wife and children – have a look to see how many carry skulls, indicating they predeceased the alderman. Anguish left a bequest when he died in 1611 to set up an educational charity that is still going to this day. Another of the church's tombs commemorates one John Symonds, who is remembered for his generosity to the poor of the parish, and whose monument sits above the 'dole table', from which money and bread were given to supplicants. As for the stained glass, like many of Norwich's churches, much of it is 19th century, but there are two lovely 15th-century roundels, one of which is from a series showing the 'Labours of the Month' and clearly depicts a figure sheltering from the rain or 'April Showers'.

Footsteps away, St Peter Hungate is a dinky 13th-century church that has been closed for worship for many years but was converted to serve as a museum of medieval church art in 2009, although even that seems to have fallen by the wayside. It has associations with the Paston family, in particular Margaret and John Paston, who lived around the corner on Elm Hill and paid for the church's redevelopment in 1458, when the nave and transepts were rebuilt. John Paston is remembered by a memorial inside the church, where there are also a handful of medieval stained glass windows, including a beautiful east window showing portraits of the evangelists from the 15th and 16th centuries.

Address Princes Street, Norwich NR3 1AE | **Getting there** Purple Line buses to Tombland; 10–15-minute walk from the railway station | **Hours** St George Tombland April–Sept Tue & Wed 10am–noon; St Peter Hungate March–Oct Sat 10am–4pm, Sun 1–4pm | **Tip** Perhaps Norwich's finest medieval stained-glass windows are in the church of St Peter Mancroft, just off the market square (see ch. 94).

83 Salhouse Broad

Closest and one of the prettiest of the Broads

Around seven miles north-east of Norwich, Salhouse Broad is the closest of the 'Broads' of the National Park – very easy to get to either by car (the journey takes around 15 minutes) or by train: Salhouse is the first stop on the Bittern Line to the North Norfolk Coast. The Broad lies at the far end of the long straggle of Salhouse village, tucked away and secluded, yet just a 10-minute walk through the trees from the car park on the main road.

Salhouse is one of the prettiest of the northern Broads, really just a deep indent in the river Bure, from which it is separated by no more than a thin spit of land. It's the property of the local Cator family, who own much of the land south of the river Bure. The land slopes down to the water from a summer camping site to a small beach and a rank of moorings where there are boats for hire. Paths disappear into the trees, and visitors can amble about and pootle by the broad, or hire canoes and kayaks to explore on the water. You might even paddle across the Hoveton Great Broad on the far side of the river – a protected nature reserve that it's only possible to reach by water. Basically an area of woodland and swamp, you can explore it by way of a marked path, ideally spotting all manner of dragonflies, butterflies and birdlife, including herons, kingfishers, marsh harriers, and possibly even the occasional otter.

You can also reach Hoveton Great Broad from the banks of Salhouse Broads by using a regular ferry, after which you might prefer to laze about by the water: it's a terrific place for families, with a fabulous children's playground and ice creams delivered by a regular ice cream boat. It's inevitably busy during the summer months, with the moorings packed to the gills, but no less appealing for all that. Out of season, it's a real gem: the Broads at their peaceful best. It even has a platform where you can lie down and appreciate some of Norfolk's darkest skies.

Address Lower Street, Norwich NR13 6RX, www.salhousebroad.org.uk | Getting there Train to Salhouse, then at least a 30-minute walk; by car, a 15-minute drive to the car park, then a 10-minute walk | Hours Accessible 24 hours | Tip It's not far to walk from Salhouse to one of the Broads' best established local breweries, Woodfordes, where you can take a tour and visit their shop or their excellent brewery tap pub, the Fur & Feather.

84 __ Sarah Glover
Ti – more than just a drink with jam and bread

Sarah Glover is probably the most famous person you've never heard of. She's yet another example of a strong and talented 18th- or 19th-century Norwich woman, who succeeded in a world where men ruled the roost and weren't averse to adopting women's ideas as their own. Without Sarah Glover, we wouldn't have *The Sound of Music* (well, at least one of the songs from it), because she is responsible for developing the Sol-Fa system of musical notation.

A teacher by trade and training, Glover was the born in 1786, the daughter of the rector of St Lawrence, a large church on St Benedicts Street which is today sadly closed and out of commission. A plaque on the wall of the church tells Glover's story, and if you are lucky enough to gain entry you can see a memorial to her and enjoy the rest of the church, which is largely empty but nonetheless remarkable for its sheer size.

Sarah Glover specialised in music and singing, led the church choir, and founded her own school for the poor girls in Norwich. As a result, she was keen to develop better ways of helping her students to understand musical pitch without having to read music. She did this by assigning each of the notes of a musical scale to its own syllable, thus designing the Sol-Fa system we still use today, and ensuring her place in history as well as the career of Julie Andrews, who famously sang – Do, Re, Mi, Fa, So, La, Ti… all the way back to Do! – in the popular film *The Sound of Music*.

It was once believed that the Sol-Fa system was invented by John Curwen, and the two certainly knew each other and were to some extent rivals in the early part of the 19th century. But it's now widely accepted that Glover was the originator of Sol-Fa, and that this was later refined by Curwen, who, perhaps slightly out of penance, commissioned a posthumous portrait of Glover clutching her Sol-Fa ladder.

Address Church of St Lawrence, 31 St Benedicts Street, Norwich NR2 3PE | Getting there Five-minute walk from Market Place; 15–20-minute walk from the railway station | Hours Open by appointment only; phone +44 (0)7721 866425 or email kroma@thecct.org.uk to arrange access, giving as much notice as possible | Tip Sarah Glover's house still stands on nearby Pottergate, marked by a plaque. Her school was in Black Boys Yard, on Colegate, next to what is currently an Indian restaurant, The Merchants of Spice.

85 Shardlake's Norwich

Discover Norwich with a local history nut

Norwich is a patchwork of many historic periods, but the one that seems to come up more than any other is Kett's Rebellion, a violent uprising that tore the region apart during the summer of 1549, and which resonates throughout the city centre even today. Lots has been written about the rebellion but no one has captured it quite as successfully as the novelist C. J. Sansom, whose novel *Tombland* recounts events through the eyes of his fictional lawyer and amateur sleuth Matthew Shardlake.

Visiting the sights of Sansom's book is a pretty good way of getting to know Norwich at a time when it was the second most important city in the land. Two sets of troops were sent here to quell the rebellion – one led by the Earl of Northampton, who lodged at the Maids Head Hotel and was defeated on Palace Plain on 1 August, 1549, and a second led by the Earl of Warwick, who defeated the rebels at Dussindale later the same month. Local history nut Paul Dickson has put together a tour of Shardlake's Norwich that takes in everywhere from Tombland to Bishop Bridge and Kett's Heights (see ch. 49), where the rebels made their camp and besieged the city. Dickson is an affable and informed guide and his Shardlake tours start and finish at the Maids Head Hotel, concluding with a drink in its historic bar.

If you enjoy the Shardlake tour, you might want to try another Paul Dickson tour: he does a Historic Pub Tour, a Black History tour of the city, a literary tour – 'Norwich, City of Stories' – and the excellent 'Norwich on the Dark Side', which visits famous murder scenes and execution sites. His Broadland tours, too, are an excellent introduction to the National Park on Norwich's doorstep, taking in Fairhaven Water Garden and including a visit to Ranworth's church of St Helen's, where you can climb up the tower for unforgettable views of the Broads.

Address Maids Head Hotel, 20 Tombland, Norwich NR3 1LB, www.pauldicksontours.co.uk | Getting there Bus to Tombland; 15-minute walk from the railway station | Hours Paul Dickson's tours usually last up to two hours and cater for groups of up to 15–20 people; most run on a regular basis and are bookable in advance but you can organise a group tour at a time of your choosing if you wish, and it makes for a great day or evening out in the city. | Tip If you want you can prolong the 16th-century vibe by making a three-minute walk from the Maids Head to the excellent The Merchant's House on Fye Bridge, where you can enjoy a drink or spot of lunch in a secret Tudor courtyard.

86__Sir Toby's on the Market
A beer-lover's delight

There are so many great stalls on Norwich Market, especially those devoted to food and drink, that it's hard to single out a particular place. Sir Toby's is worth special mention, however, if only for its popularity and the general air of conviviality and good cheer it spreads. Not only that, it stocks around 100 craft beers and real ales from all over Norfolk and, indeed, around the world. You can either take them home or try them right there on the premises. As Sir Toby himself says, it's 'a swanky off-licence', but it's also the city centre's best open-air bar!

Opened in 2018, primarily as a shop selling craft and real ales, it's the brainchild of beer-loving duo Toby Westgarth and Dominic Burke. Toby originally planned to be a brewer, and as a result amassed a lot of beer knowledge before deciding that the brewing life wasn't for him. Following a stint at a wine retailer, he got together with Dominic and they opened their stall, which stocks beer by local Norfolk brewers and speciality beers from Germany and Belgium and beyond. It's difficult to say precisely what you'll find, as they work with small brewers and the stock is ever changing, but anyone with even a passing interest in beer is sure to find something of interest: they cater for pretty much any taste. Toby and Don also sometimes get together with local producers to brew a special ale of their own, which they sell on their stall and in a few local outlets.

Sir Toby's has since morphed into a bit of a hangout, with a short bar and a few stools encouraging punters to linger and savour their beer while chewing the fat with Tob and Dom and the team. Facing the old Guildhall, it's a friendly spot, made more so by their association with the Cocina Mia Chilean food stall behind, with whom they share a covered seating area called the 'Casita', where you can enjoy a delicious empanada with your beer.

Address Stall 182, Norwich Market, Norwich NR2 1NE, www.sirtobysbeers.co.uk | **Getting there** 10-minute walk from the railway station | **Hours** Mon–Thu 11am–7pm, Fri–Sun 11am–9pm | **Tip** Toby and Dom also run the Stanford Arms pub in Lowestoft, where they sometimes sell the beer they brew themselves, along with any number of other classy ales and homemade pizzas, all of which can be consumed to the sound of regular live music!

87__ The South Asia Collection

Unique museum and shop – in the centre of Norwich

There's a fair chance that you won't have come across anywhere quite like the South Asia Collection before. Formerly known as the 'Country & Eastern', it's a unique shop and museum rolled into one – the brainchild, and indeed life's work, of Philip and Jeannie Millward. The Millwards have devoted the last 40-odd years to not only buying, preserving and displaying applied arts and crafts mainly from the Indian sub-continent, but to selling them too. Housed in a remarkable Victorian building just around the corner from The Forum, it's a stunning and unusual space that's not to be missed.

The building was originally constructed as a Victorian roller-skating rink. Clearly far ahead of its time, this didn't last long as a business, but it's a terrific space, high and wide and impressively spanned by a series of wooden vaults. It was used as a builder's merchants for a century, until Philip and Jeannie bought it in 1993, and turned it into the labour of love it is today.

Philip and Jeannie were ex-pats in the Shah's Iran. When they were forced to leave in a hurry, they ended up in Pakistan, and became increasingly interested in what they found there. Later, antique dealers by trade, they began to collect arts and crafts from the region, and now specialise in hand-block printed textiles from India and Pakistan, rugs from Afghanistan, and all sorts of other wooden furniture and artefacts.

Only 5% of what they own is ever on display at any one time. Some of it is displayed in glass cases in the central museum space. You can just come in for a look around this, if you wish, or visit one of their regular temporary exhibitions. Around the walls and on the mezzanine floor above there's all manner of enticing plunder for sale, most at surprisingly competitive prices. If you pay a visit, be aware: museum or not, it's hard to leave without buying something!

Address 34–36 Bethel Street, Norwich NR2 1NR, www.thesouthasiacollection.co.uk |
Getting there 10-minute walk from the railway station | Hours Mon–Sat 9.30am–5pm |
Tip The Coach & Horses on Bethel Street is a really cosy nearby pub with great food – a
handy place to know about in the city centre.

88 St George Colegate

Welcoming church full of interesting memorials

With a prime position on historic Colegate, the church of St George is one of the city centre's most historic and best examples of a medieval church, situated in Coslany or 'Over the Water', and so a little more tucked away than others. Back in the 19th century this was the industrial area of Norwich, close to the river and its unloading facilities. Recently, however, it has become something of a centre for creative businesses and the hospitality businesses that tend to go with them – cafés, wine bars and a fancy restaurant or two.

Built in the mid-15th century on the site of an earlier structure, St George's remains a light and welcoming church, known for its many memorials to various Norwich noble folk – indeed, it even has a plan inside so you can check who's who. Probably the most prominent memorial is the chest tomb of one Robert Jannys, carved in terracotta by the same craftsmen who created a more famous set of memorials – to the Catholic Bedingfield family – in Oxburgh, northwest of Norwich. Jannys was a wealthy grocer and his merchant's mark can be seen on the tomb; twice mayor of Norwich, he left a great deal of money to the church – hence the memorial.

The other memorial worth seeking out is that of John Crome, the 19th-century Norfolk landscape painter who died in 1821. Easy to spot at the end of the south aisle, it's decorated with a laurel wreath and carved palette and brushes, with a bust relief of the artist in between. Crome was a founder of the Norwich School group of artists, and like his colleagues in that group, was known for his naturalistic, observational approach to painting landscapes – something most evident in his beach scenes of Great Yarmouth in the 1800s. He was well-connected too, teaching the young Elizabeth Fry to draw in the late 18th century, who was then one of the youngest offspring of the prominent Gurney banking family.

Address St George's Street, Norwich NR3 1DA | **Getting there** Cross the river on Blackfriars Bridge, follow St Georges Street from there and turn left on to Colegate – the church is immediately to your right. | **Hours** Daily Jul–Sep 10am–4pm; Oct–Jun Mon–Sat noon–2pm |
Tip St George Colegate was once in the heart of Norwich's industrial district, next door to the iron foundry of Barnard, Bishop & Barnards. One of the city's most successful 19th-century businesses, their signature roundel wittily shows four bees and can still be seen around the city and elsewhere, including the Bridewell Museum, and on the ornate gates of the Sprowston Marriott hotel on the outskirts of the city, designed by Norwich native Thomas Jeckyll.

89_St George's Distillery

Tour and taste at England's original whisky producer

Around 20 miles south-west of Norwich, it's no accident that St George's Distillery was the first place to produce English whisky in more than a century. First, it's surrounded by fields of barley. Second, and perhaps more importantly, it sits right above Breckland's chalk aquifer, from which it draws beautifully clean, tasty water, meaning that it has all the ingredients on hand that you need to make an excellent single malt whisky.

St George's was set up by local farmer and whisky-lover Andrew Nelstrop and his father in 2006, but because whisky has to be in the barrel for at least three years, they didn't actually sell their first bottle until 2009. It's fine stuff, holding its own with some of the best Scottish whiskies, and in fact set something of a trend, with whisky now made in at least half a dozen locations outside Scotland. The Nelstrops have preferred to remain relatively small, producing just 60,000 bottles a year, ranging from their popular and long-standing 'Original' and 'Smoky' varieties to an 11-year-old single cask whisky, along with various seasonal and annual limited editions. They also collaborate with nearby St Peter's Brewery to produce a whisky-flavoured beer – more delicious and more popular than it sounds!

The regular, hour-long tours of the distillery are very informal, and begin with a bit of background before taking you around the plant, following the whisky from its inception in the boiling and distilling kettles right up to the three years it spends in sherry- or bourbon-aged barrels, and the eventual bottling process. Naturally they finish up with a tasting and of course you can buy some whisky for yourself. They also run 'Create your Own Whisky' tours, in which you do lots of tasting and blend whisky according to your own taste, and 'World Whisky Tours', with tours followed by tastings of lots of whiskies from different parts of the world.

Address Harling Road, Roudham, Norwich NR16 2QW, www.englishwhisky.co.uk | Getting there By car, a 30-minute drive from central Norwich following the A11 | Hours Mon–Sat 10am–4pm, Sun 10am–3pm | Tip The nearby Angel Inn at Larling, next to the A11, is a great place to stop off after a distillery tour – a cosy old pub that has been in the same family for years and serves excellent food.

90 St Giles on the Hill
City's tallest church tower a distinctive landmark

Elegantly anchoring the end of St Giles Street, the church of St Giles on the Hill is best known for having the city's tallest church tower – 35m high, and fighting for prominence with that of the Roman Catholic cathedral just metres away across the ring road. Inside, it's one of Norwich's most welcoming churches, not only for its cosy, albeit much restored interior, but also the fact that the devoted group of volunteers means it's usually accessible!

Dating back to the late-14th century, the church is a High Anglican place of worship, and slightly older than many of Norwich's medieval churches. It's mostly 15th century, boasting a nave of slender Gothic pillars, but most of the rest of the interior is the result of substantial Victorian renovation. It does, however, hold one or two more ancient features, not least a beautiful and very distinctive vaulted 15th-century porch, a hammer-beam roof decorated with angels, a medieval font decorated with Tudor roses, and a magnificent brass eagle lectern from the 15th century, brought here when nearby St Gregory's was de-sanctified. A niche to the left of the choir shows St Giles as a hermit removing an arrow from the deer that was his constant companion. In fact, the story goes that he saved the beast from the hunt by taking the arrow himself, making him forevermore the patron saint of the disabled.

Also have a look at the 16th-century iron cage or 'cresset' in the south aisle, which was used to light a beacon at the top of the tower. It's said that this was funded by one Thomas Colton at the turn of the 15th century. Lost in the marshes one very dark night, Colton was only saved from drowning by the ringing of the church bells leading him back to higher ground and safety. The cresset was replaced in 1737 by the little cupola now in place, which rings every Sunday morning and on special occasions.

Address 75 Upper St Giles Street, Norwich NR2 1AB | **Getting there** Five-minute walk from Market Place | **Hours** Sat 10.30am–1pm; sometimes during the week as well | **Tip** A quick stroll down Cowgate from the church is a stone plaque that remembers George Borrow, author of the novels *Romany Rye* and *Lavengro* and various travel books, who worked on St Giles Street. He famously coined Norwich's nickname when he called it 'a fine old city' while gazing at it from the heights of Mousehold Heath (see ch. 58).

91_ St Gregory

Fine medieval church – with a bric-a-brac store

You approach the former parish church of St Gregory back to front, via the square off Pottergate that was formed when its churchyard was cleared in the 19th century. It's one of Norwich city centre's earliest and most impressive medieval churches, originally dating back to the 13th century, but mostly re-built during the 14th and 15th centuries. However, like so many Norwich churches, it's now a redundant structure no longer used for worship. Conversely, it's also one of the city's most accessible churches, due to its nave being occupied by an antiques and collectables store – so not only can you have a look around any time during commercial opening hours, you might even pick up a bargain!

Part of the Norwich Historic Churches Trust's group of 18 places of worship, St Gregory is one of Norwich's most beautiful churches, with a lovely high nave, lit by eight, evenly-spaced clerestory windows. It also contains a number of medieval features. The church once sported a famous brass door knocker depicting a man being swallowed by a lion, but that's now in the Norwich Castle museum (see ch. 61). You can, however, see some beautiful carved misericords from the early 15th century depicting angels, winged lions and a squatting, bearded man. There's also a pre-Reformation eagle lectern and wall paintings discovered during a 19th-century restoration that include a remarkable 4-metre-high 15th-century depiction of St George and the Dragon at the end of the north aisle, which shows St George astride a rampant horse slaying a recumbent dragon, along with a few other fragments in the south aisle.

As for the stalls, there's a wide variety, offering everything from vintage clothing to jewellery, glassware and ceramics, and of course lots of books and vinyl. Rummage away to your heart's content under the church's fine wooden-vaulted roof!

Address 2 St Gregory's Alley, Pottergate, Norwich NR2 1ER | Getting there Bus to Castle Meadow, then a five-minute walk | Hours Mon–Sat 10am–5pm, Sun 10am–4pm | Tip Another NHCT church is All Saints on Westlegate, opposite John Lewis, which is also given over to bric-a-brac and antiques.

92 St John Maddermarket

Medieval church that's full of interest

St John Maddermarket on Pottergate ('John the Baptist') is one of
the smallest of the city centre's medieval churches – an unusually
square church, topped by an elegant flint tower. It was built in the
perpendicular Gothic style in the 15th century, and has a wide nave
but no real choir to speak of. Its name comes from 'madder', the yellow flower that weavers used to make red vegetable dye, indicating
that there was a market for dyes in the area.

Inside, much of the church was renovated during the Victorian
period, including some fine stained glass. Several memorials date from
earlier years, with two to the Sotherton family, Nicholas Sotherton
and his grandson Thomas, who lived around the corner in Strangers
Hall. Dating from 1540 and 1608 respectively, each window is decorated with kneeling figures of the donor and his wife. Look out for
the beautifully realised Layer Monument, adorned with both real and
allegorical polychrome figures, which recalls a local lawyer who died
in 1600. There's also a later memorial to the Norwich School painter
Joseph Stannard, buried here with his sister and infant daughter. On
the far side of the church is the wall memorial of William Nugent
Monck, who founded the Maddermarket Theatre next door in 1921.

The church is most significant for what's not here, namely what
would have been a magnificent rood screen, fragments of which survive in the Victoria & Albert Museum. The reproductions on display
give an impression of the fine quality paintings the church is missing – depictions of the saints Agatha and William of Norwich,
St Leonard and St Catherine, donated by the wealthy merchant
Ralph Seagram. Like both Sothertons, Seagram was mayor of Norwich before his death in 1472. Look down at the floor of the nave to
see his own memorial, identifiable by his merchant's mark – one of
many superb medieval brasses in the church.

Address Pottergate, Norwich NR2 1DS | Getting there Bus to Castle Meadow, then a five-minute walk | Hours Variable, but the church is sometimes open Mon, Tue, Wed & Fri 11am–3pm | Tip Just around the corner from the church, a plaque remembers Pellegrino Mazzotti, an Italian sculptor who made his home in Norwich and worked with members of the Norwich School during the 19th century. You can see his bust of the Norwich School painter John Crome in London's National Portrait Gallery.

93 — St Julian of Norwich
'All manner of things shall be well'

The Church of St Julian is an odd sight among the council blocks and car retailers of the Rouen Road area of Norwich city centre, and perhaps the last place you'd expect to find an ancient church, let alone a shrine and centre of pilgrimage. But given the church's story, it couldn't be in a better location.

The church is believed to date to pre-Norman conquest times. Due to its position just up from the river, it's thought that the church's patron may have been St Julian the Hospitaller, patron saint of ferrymen. Much of the church was destroyed during World War II, but rebuilt and re-dedicated in favour of St Julian, the 4th-century Bishop of Le Mans.

The interior is simple: a single nave with a fine 15th-century font, carved with the figures of various saints. Through an elaborate doorway is St Julian's original cell, also reconstructed after bomb damage. Despite her ongoing influence, little is known about St Julian; even her name is uncertain. Contemporary accounts are that she lived as a hermit or anchorite, dispensing advice and counselling the sick and needy in return for donations to the church. During an illness in 1373, at the age of 30, she experienced visions of Christ. As a result, she wrote a book, which remains in print today - *Revelations of Divine Love* – claimed to be the first book written in English by a woman. A series of insights into the nature of love, evil, forgiveness and suffering, there are two versions: a short one detailing the visions, a longer one written 20 years later, recounting Julian's belief that she was a messenger from God.

Her cell is now a small chapel with a simple memorial to this unsanctified saint. It remains a place of pilgrimage, however, with Julian's writings, demonstrating the need for compassion, faith and understanding in troubled times seeming as relevant today as they were seven centuries ago.

Address St Julian's Alley, Rouen Road, Norwich NR1 1QT | Getting there Bus to Castle Meadow, then a short walk; 10–15-minute walk from the railway station | Hours Daily 8.30am–6pm | Tip St Julian's sister church is the church of St John, a short walk away at the top of Timberhill – an originally Norman foundation that is still open for worship of the High Anglican variety. It's a small 15th-century building with a bright, much re-modelled interior, and known partly for the fact that it used to be the burial ground for prisoners from the nearby castle gaol.

94 St Peter Mancroft

Majestic church, home of the 'complete peal'

Just off the south side of Norwich's wide marketplace, St Peter Mancroft is Norwich's largest church – not including the city's two cathedrals, of course. St Peter Mancroft's original construction dates back to the 11th century, although rebuilding took place in the mid-15th century. The building dominates the local area, representing a massive statement of civic pride, particularly on behalf of the medieval merchants who paid for it.

The church is a majestic open space on the inside. It is a terrific example of the Gothic perpendicular style, with slender columns reaching up towards slick vaulting. The visitor's eye is particularly drawn to the magnificent stained glass of the east end, however, where a 15th-century cartoon strip of Biblical scenes has the potential to keep observers transfixed for hours, depicting the story of Christ and various saints, such as Peter, John and Francis. Also seek out some of the church's memorials – one of the most notable of which is that of the 17th-century scientist and polymath Thomas Browne. Browne was a parishioner and is buried here, although he did not rest in peace – his skull was notoriously disinterred in error, and not replaced for years! There's also the prominent local lawyer Francis Wyndham, whose upper half is depicted as a solemn counsel in his judge's cap and judicial robes, undoubtedly sternly voicing advice he administered during the trial of Mary, Queens of Scots.

The church of St Peter Mancroft is also well known for its bells, and has a small exhibition of bell ringing on the first floor of the tower, accessible by way of a winding stone staircase. It was here that one John Garner devised a way of ringing all 14 of the church's bells without stopping or repeating – the so-called 'complete peal' – in 1715, and the church remains a centre of campanological – bell-ringing! – excellence to this day.

Address Hay Hill, Norwich NR2 1QQ | Getting there 10–15-minute walk from the railway station | Hours Mon–Sat 10.30am–3.30pm | Tip Established 15 years ago, it's easy to lose an afternoon in the next door Television & Movie Store, where you can pick up anything from a 'Better Call Saul' t-shirt to the most obscure Stars Wars merchandise ever.

95 Strangers Hall

Wealthy medieval merchant's house

Originally dating back to the early 14th century, Strangers Hall is a fabulous example of a medieval 'Great House' – basically a grand residence that was the seat of a merchant or non-military nobleman during what were Norwich's medieval and renaissance years. It was so named for Norwich's late 16th-century influx of 'strangers' – Flemish weavers and their families, some of whom are thought to have found lodgings here with wealthy families. The so-called strangers were encouraged to live and work in the city during a late 16th-century downturn in Norwich's weaving industry, and their arrival brought new techniques, colour and styles, and led to a resurgence of the city's textile trade.

Strangers Hall is a creaky, multi-faceted old place, originally the property of the 15th-century cloth merchant William Barley, and later a well-to-do grocer called Nicholas Sotherton (see ch. 92). A century on in 1659, the house was owned and occupied by Joseph Paine, who, like Sotherton, was the city's mayor at the time. The labyrinth of rooms and parlours, halls and courtyards give the best impression of how a rich Norwich merchant's house would have looked between the 15th and 18th centuries.

Inside, the Great Hall has a magnificent wooden roof, panelling and carvings decorated with Sotherton's coat of arms and a beautiful mullioned bay window, and is laid out as it would have been during Tudor times. Upstairs, various rooms and bed chambers lead eventually to the Great Chamber, furnished as it would have been during Paine's residence. Downstairs, the Georgian Dining Room conjures yet another era in the life of the building, when Stranger's Hall became the official lodgings of the assizes judges. Close by, steps lead down to the basement and the building's vaulted undercroft – probably its oldest extant feature, dating back to 1320.

Address Charing Cross, Norwich NR2 4AL, www.museums.norfolk.gov.uk | Getting there Five-minute walk from Market Place; 15–20-minute walk from the railway station | Hours Wed–Fri 10am–4pm, Sun 1–4.30pm | Tip Strangers Hall is worth visiting for its garden alone – an enclosed haven of peace in the city centre, planted with an assortment of medicinal herbs and dominated by the medieval church of St Gregory next door.

96_ Street Art
Murals that question and celebrate Norwich

Norwich is not Bristol – and Norwich's best-known creator of street art, the cryptically named Knapple, is not Banksy. But street art is as much part of the landscape here as it is in any British city, with several Norwich locations playing host to some terrific, ever-changing street art and graffiti, of which Knapple is only the most prolific exponent, along with a number of vibrant and colourful murals sanctioned by the city council.

Knapple (obviously not her real name!) is a Norwich native whose signature pineapples appear sporadically all over the city. Her work is inspired by everyday life, and she specialises in grabbing people's attention with a thought, a literary quote or an image, designed to make busy passers-by stop for a moment and think. A good place to look for Knapple's creations, along with the work of other Norwich street artists, is the gallery under St Stephen's roundabout. Knapple was involved in setting this up in 2015, with all sorts of different pieces on display in all four subways – though, ironically, some have been damaged by graffiti.

The underpass under the ring road at the end of Pottergate is also regularly decorated by the city's street and graffiti artists, and was the site of a 'Black Lives Matter' mural by Knapple that was controversially painted over by the council in 2020. The council is not all bad, though: it's been instrumental in recent years in commissioning a number of murals, which serve to both brighten up and celebrate the city centre, including both large-scale works and a number of smaller murals in Norwich's Market Place. Places to look for the big ones include St Stephens Street, where you can view Andrew Wilson's *City of Stories & Mavericks*, and Castle Street, where Virgin Money is home to *The Case for Norwich* by Derek Jackson – but keep your eyes peeled, because there are plenty of others!

Address St Stephens Street, Norwich NR1 3QL | Getting there Short walk from Norwich bus station, or a short walk from Market Place | Hours Visible 24 hours | Tip Perhaps the most striking example of street art in Norwich city centre is the former Eastern Electricity building on the river, off Duke Street, on which the artist Rory Macbeth inscribed the entire text of Thomas More's *Utopia* in white paint in 2006. The building was supposed to be demolished the following year, but for the moment it remains in place and you can view it up close by way of an entrance on Duke Street or by following the riverside path on the other side of the river.

97 Strumpshaw Fen
Among Norfolk's best RSPB reserves

A few miles beyond Brundall in the southern part of the Broads National Park, Strumpshaw Fen is the closest to Norwich of Norfolk's RSPB reserves. It's an easy place to reach from the city, because not only can you drive here in 20 minutes, but getting there by rail is also an option, alighting at either Brundall Station or Buckenham Marshes just beyond.

The nature reserve lies between the railway line and the river Yare, and is one of the best places to spot birds in this part of the Broads. There are well-maintained trails that take you through a variety of different habitats, including woodlands, meadows and marsh. Follow the path through the woodland and then along by the river into the marshy reeds and wetlands – a glorious walk by any standards, but especially lovely if the sun is shining and the birds and wildlife are active.

For those who have binoculars and plenty of patience, there are three bird hides in the reserve: one at the reception, and a further two hides elsewhere. Among the rarer birds you might be lucky enough to spot are marsh harriers, bitterns, cetti's warblers and kingfishers. Even if you don't see any of them you're sure to spot a heron, teal and lots of other ducks and redpolls in the woods. Other species to look out for include the iconic swallowtail butterfly, which you can only see in The Broads. There are also increasingly large numbers of otters, which sometimes come right up to the reception area.

If you enjoy Strumpshaw, you might also want to check out nearby Buckenham Marshes. Buckenham is not as varied or picturesque, but simply a marshy wetland, again leading down to the river Yare. There's plenty of avian activity here too, including a flock of bean geese, wigeon, lapwings, golden plovers, hen harriers and even cranes. There's also a convenient large hide from which you can hopefully observe some of this diverse wildlife.

Address Low Road, Strumpshaw, Norwich, Norfolk NR13 4HS, www.rspb.org.uk | Getting there Train to Brundall, then a 20-minute walk; from Buckenham – the next stop beyond Strumpshaw – it's a slightly shorter walk, but please note that this is a request stop! | Hours Daily dawn–dusk; visitor centre Apr–Oct 9.30am–5pm, Nov–Mar 10am–4pm | Tip From Buckenham Marshes you can follow a path through the reserve and along the river to Cantley Marshes, where you can spot more birds before jumping on the train back to Norwich.

98 Subterranean Norwich

Discover the secrets of the city below ground

In the heart of Norwich, on Castle Meadow, The Shoebox is a local social enterprise that aims to bring together members of the community through events, workshops and group activities focused on life in Norwich. It also occupies one of the most fascinating and historic buildings in the city, sitting above an ancient street that dates back to medieval times, which can be explored on regular tours.

The Shoebox takes its name from 'Ponds Foot Fitters', which occupied this site from the end of the 19th century until its closure in 2014. Ponds was an institution in a city partially built on the shoe trade. Its location was also at the centre of the wool trade in medieval times, when the street and its houses were located in the ditch that protected the castle. Part of that street is still there, hidden beneath houses that were added in the 18th century to disguise the poverty and pestilence that characterised the neighbourhood.

Tours take you down a series of steps to a portion of the street, flanked on one side by what would probably have been a wealthy wool merchant's house, where you can glimpse a huge arched undercroft. On the other side of the street, a more modest house might at one time have belonged to a weaver; this later became a lodging house of the castle wardens, giving rise to the theory that the dwelling opposite was some kind of cell or dungeon, though it was more likely a shop or commercial premises. Once upon a time these premises would have had a view of the castle, but they were covered over in the 18th century, and finally cleared as slums in the 1930s.

Tours follow the 'street' further along its meandering route below ground level, passing what might have once been a secret tunnel to the castle and a corner mound of cement, designed to create a splashback to discourage gentlemen from relieving themselves on their way home from the pub!

Address 21-23 Castle Meadow, Norwich NR1 3DH, www.theshoebox.org.uk | Getting there
Just about every bus in Norwich stops outside the Shoebox! | Hours Mon–Fri 10am–5pm |
Tip The Shoebox also runs spooky tours of the street at night, as well as walking tours that
take in some of Norwich's most historic pubs on their 'Tavern Trail Tour.'

99 Surrey House

Palladian-style HQ of city's most famous firm

Probably the largest and most impressive work in the city of late-19th-century Norwich architect George Skipper (see ch. 38), Surrey House was opened in 1905 as the official headquarters of the Norwich Union insurance company (now Aviva). The company used to reside across the street, where you can still see the NU clock attached to the building opposite, but moved over when it decided a prestige building by a big-name architect would better reflect the firm's success.

Skipper aimed high when given any commission, but really pushed the boat out for Surrey House, a Palladian-style building that takes its cue from some of Norfolk's finest country houses. Evidence of this is the magnificent stained-glass windows, ceiling frescoes and lavish marbled hall and reception. It was certainly built with state-of-the-art facilities, with electricity, rudimentary central heating, document lifts, toilets, and even separate rooms for the firm's new-fangled 'typists' to work in. The marble, though, was a bit of an accident: originally supposed to be plaster and paint, Skipper managed to divert a consignment of unwanted antico and cipollino marble destined for Westminster Cathedral.

Fringed with elegant columns, the marble reception hall focuses on a marble font that heated the room, the iron pendulum above helping to circulate the air, topped by a glass dome. Insurance being that sort of industry, the edges are fringed by 'memento mori', with motifs of hourglasses and pink marble tombstones, while upstairs there's the same sense of fatalism in the wood-panelled Board Room, with frescoes showing the signs of the zodiac and the 'Three Fates' in the centre. There's a second boardroom with a portrait of one Samuel Bignold – son of the founder – who turned the Norwich Union into the powerhouse it is today and is also remembered by a statue in one of the niches outside.

Address 8 Surrey Street, Norwich NR1 3NX | **Getting there** Five-minute walk from Market Place | **Hours** Mon–Fri 9am–5pm | **Tip** Surrey House is part of a functioning office complex and not generally open to the public, but you can peek in at the marble reception hall, and the rest of the building is sometimes accessible on tours and on Heritage Open Days. The 'island site', as they call it, is a real blend of architectural periods, all linked by a spacious glass-roofed atrium, where the Aviva workers have their lunch.

100 Thomas Browne

City's brainiest man sits amid pigeons and buskers

The church of St Peter Mancroft on Norwich's market place (see ch. 94) is the final resting spot of Thomas Browne, a 17th-century polymath who is best known for his *Religio Medici* ('The Religion of a Doctor') – a meditation on everything from religion to science, alchemy and astrology. His tomb, in front of the church's high altar, is marked by a memorial plaque, although in fact Browne had wanted to be cremated, anxious that his bones might be disinterred – which is exactly what happened! His skull was taken from his grave and displayed in a doctor's surgery for almost a century, and only put back in 1922.

Browne is commemorated on the nearby square of Haymarket, where he contemplates a broken urn in his right hand while pigeons perch on top of his head. At his feet lie a litter of stone stools and benches, and a suitably massive brain referencing his various works, usually to a soundtrack of the buskers on Gentleman's Walk. It's a slightly tawdry spot for someone who was one of the greatest minds of his age, surrounded by high street chains, but it's one of Norwich's busiest spots, always crowded with pedestrians. In any case, he may have been happy to be so close to his house, which stood at the junction of Haymarket and Orford Place, and is marked by a plaque.

Browne wrote a number of other philosophical discourses over the years, perhaps most notably *Urn Burial*, a book about burial customs, and its sequel, *The Garden of Cyrus*, which contemplates the five-point pattern of the 'quincunx' in nature. He is also credited with having coined a number of words still in use – for example electricity, pathology, even computer! Spending his later years in Norwich, he was much admired by a more recent Norwich thinker, Max Sebald, who called him 'the writer's writer', and whose poetic and thoughtful, meandering yet learned prose made him his natural successor.

Address Haymarket, Norwich NR2 1QD | Getting there Short walk from Market Place | Hours Always open | Tip The building on the site of Browne's old house is actually a rather distinguished one, home now to a Pret a Manger but designed as Haymarket Chambers in 1901 for a local grocer, by the iconic Norwich architect George Skipper.

101 Thorpe Marshes
A taste of the Broads without leaving the city

Norwich sits on the western-most edge of the Broads National Park, and Thorpe Marshes is another place where it's possible to get a taste of its unique landscape without having to leave the city. Sandwiched between Yarmouth Road and the river Yare in the suburban Norwich neighbourhood of Thorpe St Andrew, the 25 hectares of this Norfolk Wildlife Trust nature reserve is one of eight within the city's boundaries. Established just over a decade ago, it provides an in-a-nutshell glimpse of Broadland. It even has its own broad – St Andrew's Broad – well-marked riverside walks, and an area of reedy marshes that attracts all manner of birdlife.

A short walk down Whitlingham Lane, over the railway bridge, and you're there. You can either do a shortish walk down to and along the river and around the broad, or take a slightly longer – and often muddier! – alternative route that takes in more of the marshes, dykes and drainage ditches beyond the St Andrew's Broad. Of the wildlife in the area, look out for cetti's warblers, stonechats and reed buntings, and pochards, gadwalls, herons and great crested grebes on the water, as well as lots of beautiful dragonflies and damselflies, and the brown Norfolk hawker dragonfly, which thrives in the watery landscape of The Broads.

Thorpe Marshes is a peaceful spot, only slightly marred by the constant drone of the A47 just beyond. There are benches where visitors can sit for contemplation and birdwatching, and the paths are all well signposted, and most of them accessible. However, unlike many broads, the water is deep, and swimming here can be dangerous – indeed it was the site of a shocking tragedy a few years ago, when two teenagers died after getting into trouble in the water. Their names are commemorated on one of the benches – adding a melancholy air to what is otherwise a thoroughly uplifting walk.

Address Thorpe St Andrew, Norwich NR7 0QA | Getting there Green Line buses 14 and 15 run past Thorpe Marshes | Hours Always open | Tip A perfect way to finish off a walk through Thorpe Marshes is to stop for a pint, a glass of wine or a meal at the 16th-century Rushcutters Arms, a five-minute walk away by the river in Thorpe St Andrew.

102___Tombland

The beating heart of Norwich in Anglo-Saxon times

It seems morbidly named, but the name of the triangular open space of Tombland, anchored at one end by the Maids Head hotel, and on one side by the grounds of the cathedral, is simply derived from the Anglo-Saxon word for 'empty space' – when it was the principal marketplace of the pre-Norman settlement. Even after that it remained an important spot, but the market moved to its current location, and Tombland gradually became more central to the city's historic and ecclesiastical background than its commercial life – albeit one that still throbs with traffic and people.

It was home for many years to the city's mayors, who lived in the rather grand merchant's house opposite the cathedral, known for years as 'Samson and Hercules', due to the pair of figures support-ing its porch. The building itself dates from 1657, and the figures were added by the mayor of the time. They were later relocated to the courtyard at the rear, but returned to the front of the building in the late 19th century, after which the building became a popular enter-tainment venue and gained its exotic nickname.

On one side of the house, the Louis Marchesi pub remembers the founder of the Round Table movement, formed here in the 1920s. On the other side is the so-called Augustine Steward House (see ch. 7), which dates back to 1530; famously crooked, it's said to have been used for negotiations during the Kett Rebellion. Steward him-self was a well-to-do local merchant who served as mayor, and funded many of the city's buildings in the 16th century. He died in 1571, and is buried in nearby St Peter Hungate, but his merchant's mark is still visible on the corner of the building. The only way to gain access is to visit the 'Cryptic Escape' escape room on its lower floors. Failing that, take a walk through Tombland Alley to admire it from the out-side, and follow the path past the church of St George.

Address Tombland, Norwich NR3 1HF | Getting there Purple Line buses to Tombland; 10–15-minute walk from the railway station | Hours 24 hours | Tip Perhaps the most significant feature on Tombland is in fact part of the cathedral – Erpingham Gate – a decorative arch into the cathedral close that was built in 1420. Carved with the statues of male and female saints, at its centre is the kneeling figure of local landowner Thomas Erpingham, a hero of Agincourt who paid for the gate and was one of the most powerful men in England at the time.

103 Tombland Books

Tardis-like home of literary treasures

Browsing and buying in Norwich's many used bookshops is a real pleasure for any bookworm in the city, and there are plenty of places to do so. Perhaps the city centre's best, however, is Tombland Books – a classic used bookstore which occupies a timbered building opposite the cathedral. Tombland's Tardis-like interior is choc-a-block with some 30,000 books on display, and if that wasn't enough for a keen book buyer to choose from, there are another 100,000 or so in stock. It's a genuine treasure trove for book-lovers, and it's easy to lose a few hours here among the stacks.

Tombland has been called 'the Best Book Shop in East Anglia' by the popular used bookshop guide, Drif's, and is considered one of the dozen best in the UK – and it's easy to see why. The shop has been operating for over three decades, and stocks everything from classic Penguin paperbacks to antiquarian hardbacks. There are books on every subject imaginable, ranging from local history, art and architecture to travel, biography and of course all kinds of fiction. Tombland will also try to find a particular book you're looking for if they don't have it, and will even repair and bind that favourite much-read classic if it's beginning to fall apart.

There are some real gems to be had in Tombland Books if you're prepared to scour the shelves for long enough. And that shouldn't be too much of a chore, because searching the shelves is part of the pleasure of this shop. Tombland also has an online catalogue, and you can fill in a search form to access stock not displayed in the store. But just in case you can't find what you want, there's another used bookshop close by, on Elm Hill: the rather sweetly named Dormouse Books. This is quite a lot smaller than Tombland Books but is good on first editions and rare books, and has a good stock on the Broads and Norfolk generally.

More books upstairs on our top floor

Address 8 Tombland, Norwich NR3 1HF, +44 (0)1603 490000, tomblandbookshop.co.uk | **Getting there** Purple Line buses to Tombland; 10−15-minute walk from the railway station | **Hours** Tue−Sat 10am−4.30pm | Tip Norwich has a third used bookshop on the other side of the city centre − J. R. & R. K. Ellis − which stocks more mainstream titles. Try also the excellent City Books, just off the Market on Davey Place, which has a terrific selection of books on Norwich and Norfolk, plus lots more besides.

104__ Trowse Newton

Built by the Colmans for mustard factory workers

It's only just over a mile south of Norwich's centre, but Trowse (or to give it its full name, Trowse Newton) feels like a place apart from the rest of the city – a separate village on the other side of the Yare and Tas rivers that sits right on the edge of open country, and marks the southernmost point of Norwich, with only the traffic buzz of the A 47 just beyond.

The village has been here a long time, as the ruins at nearby Whitlingham Country Park attest, along with the church of St Andrew on the main road through the village – a pretty flint church built in 1281, which retains a window from the same period. Most of Trowse, though, is of more recent vintage, developed in the 19th century as a 'model village' to house workers from the nearby Colmans mustard factory. The Colmans lived at nearby Crown Point Hall – now Whitlingham Hall – which was acquired by Jeremiah Colman in 1865, and is now an apartment complex. There's a uniformity to some of the housing, and although some of the development here is more recent – for example the crescent of Dutch gables at the end of the main street – Trowse is one of the few survivors of the glory days of the Colmans in this part of the town. The factory itself sadly closed in 2019, after 160 years on the same site.

There are lots of nice things about Trowse: it's close to the city centre but fiercely independent of it (the result of a 2008 referendum here was overwhelmingly to remain separate from Norwich); it's handy for green spaces like Whitlingham Country Park, and has an appealing centre with lots of amenities that's very peaceful and self-contained since they re-directed the A146 30 years ago. There are a couple of pubs – the Crown Point Tavern and the White Horse – and a well-known vegetarian restaurant, and it even boasts a dry ski slope for those who are so inclined.

Address Trowse, Norwich NR14 8SZ | Getting there Bus 40A to Trowse Primary School | Hours Always open | Tip Stop off for a beer at the taproom and garden of the Redwell Brewery which specialises in low volume, gluten-free and vegan craft ales that you can consume along with Vault pizzas cooked on premises.

105 University of East Anglia
Crazy architecture and Nobel prize-winning alumni

Occupying around 270 acres on the western fringes of the city, the University of East Anglia (UEA) was founded in a major 1960s expansion of the UK's universities and quickly gained a reputation for radicalism. Along with its contemporaries – Essex, Kent, Sussex, York and one or two others – it saw regular sit-ins, freak-outs and political happenings that were thoroughly in tune with the spirit of the age.

Nowadays it's a sleepier place altogether, but the radicalism of some of its architecture remains – for example the Norfolk Terrace and Suffolk Terrace halls of residence, designed in the shape of ziggurats by Denys Lasdun and a stark contrast to the bucolic nature of their location, which, like much of the campus, overlooks green open spaces and the university's very own lake or 'broad'. Nearby, you can also see the first of Norman Foster's many public buildings, and the shed-like Sainsbury Centre for Visual Arts – not only an auspicious gallery in its own right, but also home to the university history of art department (see ch. 81). Opposite, the elegant curves of Constable Terrace represent another prestigious piece of modern architecture, this one added by Rick Mather in 1991. Finally, there's 'The Square', the hub of the university campus, designed by local architect Bernard Feilden, who took over and refined Lasdun's plans, adding this stepped open space to encourage sociability. He also fixed Norwich's wonky cathedral spire.

The university is perhaps best known for its pioneering Creative Writing MA. Founded by Malcolm Bradbury and Angus Wilson in 1970 for 'writers of originality and potential', it set the template for the many creative writing courses that have followed, and is still held to be one of the best in the country. Over the years it's produced a number of highly successful writers, including novelists Rose Tremain, Ian McEwan and the winner of the 2017 Nobel Prize for Literature, Kazuo Ishiguro.

Address Norwich NR4 7TJ | Getting there Blue Line buses 25 and 26 to UEA | Hours
24 hours | Tip Nearby Earlham Hall was the seat of the rich and influential Gurney family
and the childhood home of Elizabeth Fry. It became part of UEA when it opened in
1963 and now houses its law department, but you can still visit the adjacent park which
sweeps down to the banks of Yare. Have a cuppa at its little café and cross the road to follow
the Yare Valley Path, which starts across the road by the church of St Mary, following the
river as its bends around into Bowthorpe Marshes.

106__ Unthank Road

Norwich's coolest residential street?

The main artery of Norwich's so-called 'Golden Triangle', Unthank Road is a long, mainly residential thoroughfare linking the edge of the centre with the city's eastern fringes. It's home to a large stock of medium-sized terraced and semi-detached houses that were added during the building boom of the late 19th century and have remained popular with the upwardly mobile middle classes ever since due to their size and location.

The road is named after the family instrumental in the development of this part of town, who arrived in Norwich from the northeast in the late 18th century. The family patriarch, William Unthank, was a stage coach operator, and his son, also called William, was a solicitor – a winning combination that led to them acquiring a large amount of land in the area. Legend has it that what is now Unthank Road was no more than a dirt path when William's son Clement rode along it to woo his future wife, who lived further out of town – and that is how the road got its name.

Most Norwich folk think of 'Colonel Unthank' in relation to Unthank Road. He was thought to be Clement's son – also called Clement – and a captain in the 17th Lancers and the Norfolk Volunteer Regiment. He oversaw the road's development by selling off land to developers in the 19th century – a process that was only hastened by the arrival of a tram service in the early 1900s. Nowadays, Unthank Road is a by-word for Norwich's most gentrified district, home not only to artisan bakers and coffeeshops, but also to students, young families and just about anyone else looking for an affordable, convenient place to live. Naturally, its popularity has spawned a host of lively local hospitality businesses, particularly on the stretch from Park Lane to Warwick Street, with funky pubs like the Pear Tree Inn and cool restaurants such as Blue Joanna.

Address Norwich NR2–NR4 | Getting there Blue Line bus 25 runs along Unthank Road | Hours Accessible 24 hours | Tip Perhaps the most enduring legacy of Colonel Unthank is long-time resident Clive Lloyd's excellent long-running blog – www.colonelunthanksnorwich.com – which regularly deep-dives into the minutiae of Norwich history, buildings, art and trivia.

107 __ W. G. Sebald's Grave

One of literature's 'most transformative figures'

The churchyard of this tiny round-towered church, dedicated to St Andrew and originally of Saxon origin, feels very far away from Norwich despite being so close. Apart from the church itself, the main reason most people come here is to visit the grave of W. G. – 'Max' – Sebald, a writer and academic at UEA, who died accidentally in 2001 at the relatively young age of 57. Sebald is buried close to where he lived and died, when his car collided with a lorry after he suffered a sudden heart attack.

Sebald was a unique writer, indeed, he virtually invented his own genre, which he called 'documentary fiction'. He wrote mainly about the past but not in the conventional sense, mixing elements of travel writing, modern history and personal observations to make his books compelling, shape-shifting narratives. The text would hop from one subject to another, sometimes blurring fact and fiction, but always in Sebald's distinctively impersonal, slightly melancholic style. Uniquely, he sometimes also incorporated photos into his texts. Before his death, he was said to be under consideration for the Nobel Prize for Literature, despite his relatively limited output.

As a German writer and academic who made his home in Norfolk, Sebald was to some extent a citizen of nowhere, which made him particularly qualified to comment on how the present and past entwine, and how they sometimes appear to the detached observer. His final resting place is a lovely spot – very peaceful, in what is almost the archetypal Norfolk country churchyard. It's particularly suited to a writer who was fascinated by the historical nooks and crannies of the region and its landscape, for example in his most East Anglian book, *The Rings of Saturn*, which picks apart the history and landscape of the Suffolk coast. His headstone sits at the far end of the church, just by the curve of the apse.

Address St Andrew's churchyard, Framingham Earl, Norwich NR14 7SD | Getting there By car, a 20-minute drive from central Norwich, following the A146 out of the city towards Lowestoft; bus X22 can drop you on the main road, then a 15-minute walk | Hours 24 hours | Tip St Andrew's is not often open, which is a pity, because it has various interesting features inside, including two medieval stained glass windows, one in the north side of the nave, showing St Catherine with her wheel, and the other in the tower depicting St Margaret according to her legend, bursting out of a red dragon.

108 Wheatfen Nature Reserve

'A breathing space for the cure of souls'

Norwich is the only city in the country to sit within the boundaries of a national park, and as a result it's not very difficult to access the beauties of The Broads, indeed even its most peaceful and unadulterated corners lie within easy reach of the city centre. One such example is Wheatfen Broad, home to a nature reserve initiated by a local naturalist called Ted Ellis. Ellis lived here with his wife Phyllis in a thatched marshman's cottage by the entrance, and is still known as one of the most vocal champions of the beauty of the Norfolk Broads and the need to preserve it for future generations.

Ellis was keeper of the natural history collection at Norwich Castle (see ch. 61) from 1928 to 1956, when he began writing nature features for the Eastern Daily Press; later he appeared on television nature programmes, becoming something of a local celebrity and an advocate for the preservation of the unique landscape of Norfolk, which he called 'a breathing space for the cure of souls'. Ellis died in 1986, after which Wheatfen's marshes and dykes were turned into a nature reserve, ironically one of the national park's least-visited spots, yet one where it's possible to see some of the wildlife stars of The Broads – marsh harriers, herons, swallowtail butterflies, lots of damselflies and dragonflies, and if you're lucky even a kingfisher or two.

A series of paths lead from the entrance down to the river Yare – about an hour's walk there and back. Following these gives some appreciation of what Ted saw in this place, with its reed beds, fens and little broads. He is buried on the high ground by the ruined Norman church in nearby Church Farm Nature Reserve. Phyllis, meanwhile, lived here until her death in 2004, and was just as much of an advocate of nature as her husband, setting up the Ted Ellis Trust and receiving an MBE in 1996.

Address The Covey, Surlingham, Norfolk NR14 7AL | Getting there By car, a 25-minute drive from central Norwich, taking the A146 out of the city and then turning left on the other side of the A47 towards Kirby Bedon | Hours Daily 8am–6pm, but it's usually always open | Tip After seeing Wheatfen, you can do a fairly easy circular walk towards the river at Surlingham, doubling back to take in Ted Ellis's grave near Church Farm, then maybe a pint and a bite at the riverside Ferry House.

109 Whitlingham Country Park

The National Park on Norwich's doorstep

On the south-eastern edge of the city, Whitlingham Country Park extends from the junction of the Yare and Wensum rivers, a mixture of water and wetlands, woods and meadows. One of the most popular outdoor attractions in the area, at its centre are two large lakes or 'Broads', formed relatively recently from disused gravel pits. Though not strictly speaking part of The Broads National Park, they provide about as good an introduction as you could wish for to the beauty of the wetlands that lie beyond, yet they are easy to reach and have low key appeal all of their own.

Just beyond the old Colman's mustard factory, Whitlingham is a rather sprawling area, encompassing a small village of the same name, the banks of the river Yare and the ruins of the former Trowse Newton Hall, which was a country home of the priors of Norwich Cathedral, and later home to an eccentric character called John Money. Managed by the Whitlingham Charitable Trust, the park is a popular place to stroll and discover nature, with opportunities to spot herons, kingfishers and cormorants, otters and bats, as well as more run-of-the-mill grebes, swans and ducks.

There are woodland trails and footpaths all over, including a two-mile accessible trail all the way around the Great Broad. On the way you can stop off at the Outdoor Education Centre, where the emphasis is on all things watery – canoeing and kayaking, sailing and windsurfing. Just beyond is the meeting point of no fewer than three rivers – the Tas, Wensum and Yare – a formerly sacred spot that was marked by a wooden 'Henge' that framed the setting sun. There's also a café – the Flint Barn – for less energetic types, and Whitlingham is popular with cyclists too, not least because National Cycle Route 1 runs through the site.

Address Whitlingham Lane, Norwich NR14 8TR | Getting there Bus to Whitlingham Lane; by car, a 10-minute drive from the city centre | Hours 24 hours | Tip Those wanting to enjoy Whitlingham a bit longer can stay at the excellent Whitlingham Broad Campsite, which as well as regular camping pitches has pre-pitched bell tents, shepherd's huts and magnificent woodland dens.

110__Wymondham Abbey

Impressive church and medieval ruins

Just 10 miles south-west of Norwich you'll find located the small but pleasant town of Wymondham (pronounced 'Windam'). Wymondham is famous as the place where Robert and William Kett instigated the peasants' revolt of 1549 – an event that culminated with the encampment being positioned outside Norwich on Mousehold Heath, and eventually led to Kett's imprisonment and execution at Norwich Castle (see ch. 61). It's worth the short trip from the city to visit the remains of Wymondham's Benedictine abbey, which sprawl across the flat riverside meadows at one end of the high street, next to the town's large, double-towered church.

The abbey was founded at the beginning of the 12th century, and modelled on what was then the brand-new cathedral at Norwich. As well as being a Benedictine monastery, the abbey has always doubled as Wymondham's parish church, which it remains to this day. Over the years this has led to some rather complicated squabbles between the townsfolk and the church, however. These disagreements once even involved the Pope, and led to the building of the second, west tower, which was added for the benefit of the parishioners in the 1490s. After the abbey's dissolution under Henry VIII, the church fell into disrepair, and the area became a focus for the protests against the land enclosures of the mid-1500s.

A plaque marks the spot where Robert Kett's brother, William, was strung up on the west tower, while inside, the church sports a lovely Norman nave of grey stone arches supporting a wooden beamed roof decorated with over 70 carved angels. The choir of the church was destroyed along with the cloister and other buildings during the Reformation. Also check out the vividly gilded altar screen, an enormous creation dating from the early 1900s, that is widely regarded as the finest work by the neo-Gothic Scottish architect John Ninian Comper.

Address Church Street, Wymondham, Norwich NR18 0PH | **Getting there** By car, a 25-minute drive to Wymondham from the centre of Norwich; Turquoise Line bus 13 | **Hours** Mon–Sat 10am–3pm, Sun noon–1pm | **Tip** Other things to see in Wymondham include the Market Cross at the top of the high street, the Heritage Museum, housed in the town's old prison, and the creaky old Green Dragon pub near the abbey, where Robert Kett himself might have supped an ale or two.

111_ Yalm

The spirit of north-west food halls in Norwich

Under new owners, Norwich's Royal Arcade (see ch. 78) is looking better than it has for some time, attracting better businesses and seeing increased footfall. There's no better example of this new broom than Yalm, a bustling double-decker food hall that opened at the end of 2022, and has been busy ever since.

Situated in premises vacated by Jamie's Italian before the pandemic, Yalm is channelling a funky foodiness that has infiltrated Norwich in recent years – in the Market, The Lanes, and in some great small businesses that are flourishing in NR3. The food hall is a lockdown baby, set up by Dan Searle, whose Scandinavian-style outdoor food court (Mysa Bar) in Castle Gardens, was just the ticket for hungry city folk eager to get out. Dan had no real track record in food, but Mysa Bar was so popular that he was encouraged to try it indoors, and the Royal Arcade provided the perfect opportunity. Why Yalm? Well, Dan is Norwich born-and-bred and 'Yalm' – he assures us! – is an old Norfolk word that means 'to eat hungrily' – which you'll realise is spot-on when you walk in here. Basically, he has assembled a collection of some of the best food businesses in Norfolk, carefully curated and all in one place.

Immediately by the ground floor entrance, there's a counter serving coffee and pastries, across the way from a sushi-style bar with a conveyor belt transporting all sorts of scrummy cheese and charcuterie items past peckish punters – perfect for enjoying with a glass of wine before you move upstairs for the main event, where half a dozen kitchens and a bar surround a central eating area. It's a tempting collection, and your tastebuds will be buzzing as you choose from pizza, Mexican food, Middle Eastern-flavoured delights and more. Have a browse, settle down, fire up the App and place your order. It's hard to decide, but that's just the point. You'll be back!

Address 23–24 Royal Arcade, Norwich NR2 1NQ | Getting there Bus to Castle Meadow; 10–15-minute walk from the railway station | Hours Tue–Sat 8am–11pm, Sun 9am–6pm | Tip Dan Searle's other place in central Norwich is the Rumsey Welles pub, five minutes' walk away on Charing Cross, a terrific and very convivial pub where they serve good ales and all sorts of excellent pies, and sometimes host live music and DJs in their basement bar.

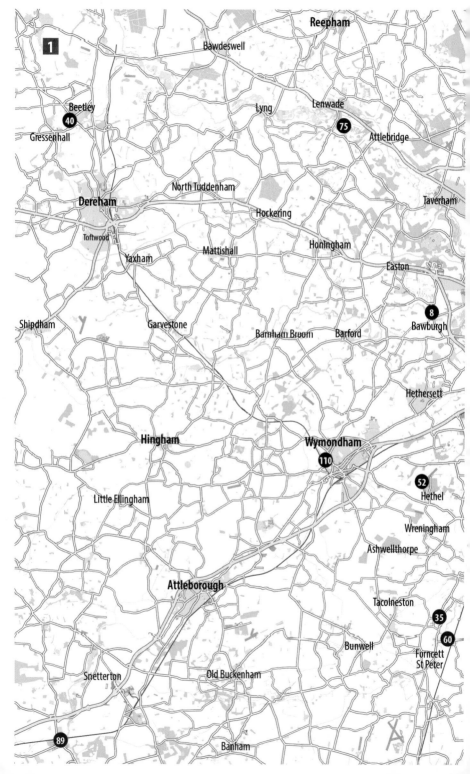

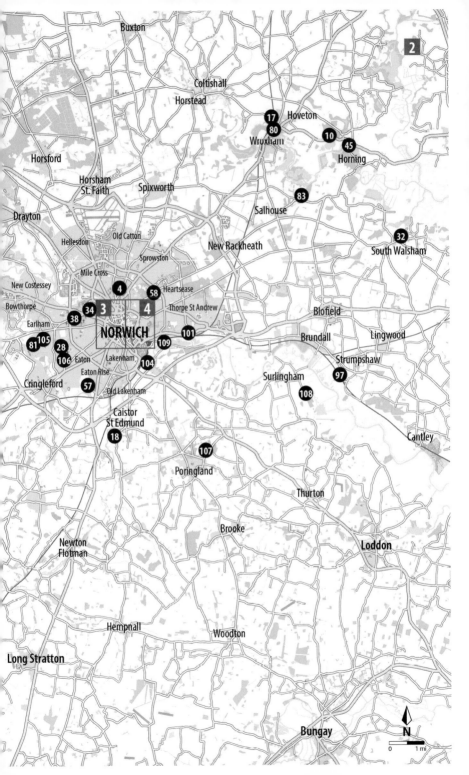

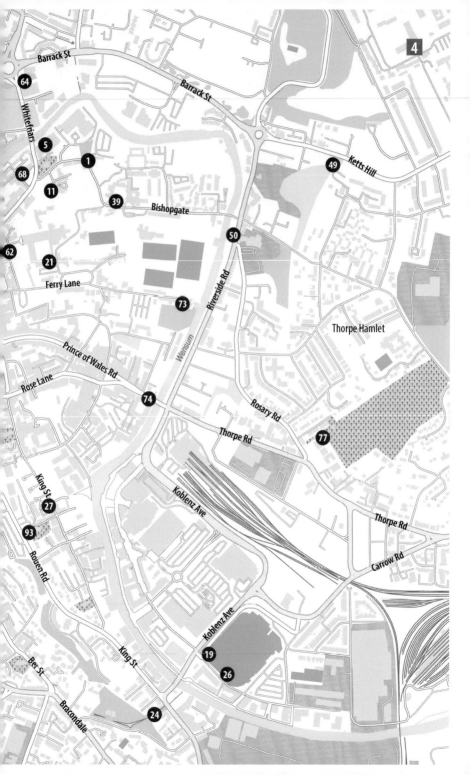

Barrack St

Barrack St

64

Whitefriars

5

1

68

11

39

Bishopgate

49

Ketts Hill

50

62

21

Ferry Lane

73

Riverside Rd

Wensum

Thorpe Hamlet

Prince of Wales Rd

Rose Lane

74

Rosary Rd

Thorpe Rd

77

King St

27

Koblenz Ave

Thorpe Rd

93

Carrow Rd

Rouen Rd

Ber St

King St

Koblenz Ave

Bracondale

24

19

26

Solange Berchemin,
Martin Dunford, Karin Tearle
111 Places in Greenwich
That You Shouldn't Miss
ISBN 978-3-7408-1107-5

Ed Glinert, Marc Zakian
111 Places in London's East End
That You Shouldn't Miss
ISBN 978-3-7408-0752-8

John Sykes, Birgit Weber
111 Places in London
That You Shouldn't Miss
ISBN 978-3-7408-1644-5

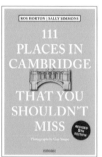

Rosalind Horton, Sally Simmons,
Guy Snape
111 Places in Cambridge
That You Shouldn't Miss
ISBN 978-3-7408-1285-0

Phil Lee, Rachel Ghent
111 Places in Nottingham
That You Shouldn't Miss
ISBN 978-3-7408-1814-2

Ben Waddington, Janet Hart
111 Places in Birmingham
That You Shouldn't Miss
ISBN 978-3-7408-1350-5

Ed Glinert, David Taylor
111 Places in Yorkshire
That You Shouldn't Miss
ISBN 978-3-7408-1167-9

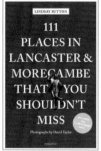

Lindsay Sutton, David Taylor
111 Places in Lancaster
and Morecambe
That You Shouldn't Miss
ISBN 978-3-7408-1996-5

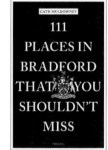

Cath Muldowney
111 Places in Bradford
That You Shouldn't Miss
ISBN 978-3-7408-1427-4

Kim Revill, Alesh Compton
111 Places in Leeds
That You Shouldn't Miss
ISBN 978-3-7408-0754-2

Michael Glover, Richard Anderson
111 Places in Sheffield
That You Shouldn't Miss
ISBN 978-3-7408-1728-2

Julian Treuherz,
Peter de Figueiredo
111 Places in Manchester
That You Shouldn't Miss
ISBN 978-3-7408- 1862-3

Julian Treuherz,
Peter de Figueiredo
111 Places in Liverpool
That You Shouldn't Miss
ISBN 978-3-7408-1607-0

David Taylor
111 Places in Newcastle
That You Shouldn't Miss
ISBN 978-3-7408-1043-6

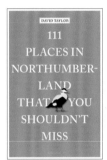

David Taylor
111 Places in Northumberland
That You Shouldn't Miss
ISBN 978-3-7408-1792-3

David Taylor
111 Places along Hadrian's Wall
That You Shouldn't Miss
ISBN 978-3-7408-1425-0

Katherine Bebo, Oliver Smith
111 Places in Poole
That You Shouldn't Miss
ISBN 978-3-7408-0598-2

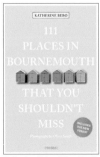

Katherine Bebo, Oliver Smith
111 Places in Bournemouth
That You Shouldn't Miss
ISBN 978-3-7408- 1166-2

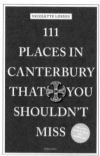

Nicolette Loizou
**111 Places in Canterbury
That You Shouldn't Miss**
ISBN 978-3-7408-0899-0

Rob Ganley, Ian Williams
**111 Places in Coventry
That You Shouldn't Miss**
ISBN 978-3-7408-1044-3

Martin Booth, Barbara Evripidou
**111 Places in Bristol
That You Shouldn't Miss**
ISBN 978-3-7408-2001-5

Martin Booth, Barbara Evripidou
**111 Places for Kids in Bristol
That You Shouldn't Miss**
ISBN 978-3-7408-1665-0

Alexandra Loske
**111 Places in Brighton and
Lewes That You Shouldn't Miss**
ISBN 978-3-7408-1727-5

Justin Postlethwaite
**111 Places in Bath
That You Shouldn't Miss**
ISBN 978-3-7408-0146-5

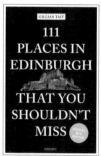

Gillian Tait
**111 Places in Edinburgh
That You Shouldn't Miss**
ISBN 978-3-7408-1476-2

Tom Shields, Gillian Tait
**111 Places in Glasgow
That You Shouldn't Miss**
ISBN 978-3-7408-1863-0

Gillian Tait
**111 Places in Fife
That You Shouldn't Miss**
ISBN 978-3-7408-1740-4

I'm thankful to so many people for sharing their love and knowledge of Norwich while writing this book. Discovering so much more about the city than I thought possible has been a joy, but meeting its current denizens has been the biggest pleasure of all, and I'm immensely grateful for their time and their passion for this unique city. In no particular order, thanks to Melanie Cook, Rupert and Joy Hipwell, Simon and Alex Egan, Dave Ansell, Paul Dickson, Caroline and Ian Johnson, Peter and Alex Howe, John Campbell, Phil Lee, Solange Berchemin, Caroline Osborne for Jenny Lind, and many more too numerous to mention. Big thanks are also due to Martin Sketchley for editing the book, Laura Olk for her sage guidance and above all to Karin Tearle, not only for her wonderful photos but also her friendship, patience and enthusiasm in sometimes difficult circumstances. Finally, nothing makes me happier than exploring Norwich's nooks and crannies with Caroline, Daisy and Lucy, and of course Sonny – thank you!

Martin Dunford is one of the founders of the international travel guide series Rough Guides. He is the author of more than 10 guidebooks and was the publisher of Rough Guides for many years, before going on to found the specialist UK travel and accommodation website www.coolplaces.co.uk. Martin also works as a freelance travel writer, writing regularly about the UK, Belgium, Holland and Italy, among other destinations, and as a consultant. Finally he is a trustee of the Norfolk charity, The Broads Trust, working regularly with tourism businesses in the Broads National Park.

Karin Tearle has a BA in French and Italian from Goldsmiths, University of London and lived in Bordeaux, France for several years before returning to the UK to have a family. She is a trustee of the Rwanda Development Trust which funds small capacity-building projects and was interpreter for the BBC World Service for a programme about the 1994 genocide. Karin has retained her links with the country and continues to work with the Rwandese. She also manages a listed building in Greenwich and has an affinity with this historic town where she has lived for thirteen years. Karin is social secretary of Aperture Woolwich Photographic Society, one of the oldest clubs in the country and is extremely passionate about photography.

The information in this book was accurate at the time of publication, but it can change at any time. Please confirm the details for the places you're planning to visit before you head out on your adventures.